Living Your
DREAM CAREER

DO what
you LOVE

LOVE what
you DO

GET A JOB – KEEP A JOB – LEVEL-UP – DON'T MESS UP

Written by Dr. Scott Dell and Dr. AnnaMaria Bliven

Living Your
DREAM CAREER

Dr. Scott Dell

Dr. AnnaMaria Bliven

ISBN-13: 979-8-86062-368-2

DEDICATION

Dedicated to our friends, colleagues, families, students, and fellow veterans.

We're in this together. Helping to make a better world by providing opportunities for all to share, learn, and grow together. It is our hope and passion that by providing resources for those pursuing their dreams, our contribution will foster happiness and success.

The journey is the reward. Thank you for committing to your own personal and professional growth and joining us on this journey.

To YOUR Success

TABLE OF CONTENTS

ACKNOWLEDGMENTS

We appreciate the supreme support of our families in giving us the opportunity to dedicate the time and resources to the development of this book, workbook, course, along with our Future Forward Academy team. We wish to acknowledge the inspiration and encouragement received from our career service colleagues in the pursuit of making a difference in the lives of others. We also want to thank our students, who through their own desire to grow while pursuing their passions, have inspired us to want to provide tools and resources that can assist them in reaching their maximum success.

PREFACE

"Do you know what you want to be when you grow up?" is a common question most of us hear early in life. The answer to this question comes from deep within us. Our passions are developing over time, and the way we discover what they are is to observe ourselves and see what the moments are when we "light up" and become "more alive and engaged."

Our deeply rooted "why" needs to be discovered along the journey of life. Though the paths might change, the root of our direction is based on following the things we care about. Understanding this allows us to follow the direction of our "life's compass." So often we hear people say, "I am not sure what I want to be when I grow up. What that really means is that we need to take a breath, be present, and be observant when the moments come when we are happy, satisfied, and fulfilled with whatever is taking place at that time. As you are reading this, can you remember when you felt happy, satisfied, and fulfilled in life? Was that just a minute ago, a year ago, or never?

This textbook is meant to help you discover your "life's compass, "and then use this compass to design a pathway that makes perfect sense for YOU. The real YOU. This is who you are deep down. This is your TRUE NATURE, not someone you had to become due to situations and circumstances. Rest assured, if your pathway is one that someone else created for you, there is a way to get on track and sync it with your own. This textbook will help you do that.

"Where there is a will, there is a way." No matter where you find yourself in your life today, there is a way to get on track with the perfect pathway that makes sense for your today and tomorrow. The resources here provide you with tools to help you point your personal compass in the right direction and lead you to find your "North Star."

Your "North Star" is the type of career you may want to have that best aligns with your core self. It's about YOUR personal growth and ultimate fulfillment - the things that make you happy and that you can commit your energies to with vigor. This is a career that matches your dreams, goals, desires, abilities, passions, and personality.

When you are working a job that allows YOU TO SHINE with all that you are, you are no longer working, you are contributing with the added benefit of compensation. When you are no longer working but instead contributing with compensation, you are loving what you do and doing what you love. When that happens, YOU LOVE MONDAY MORNINGS, Tuesdays, and Wednesdays…!

Too many people go through their life stuck in a job or position they hate. By taking advantage of the resources and opportunities within this textbook, doing the exercises, and following through, you will **not be** one of those "stuck" people. The exercises are designed to help you:

- Discover your life's compass.
- See your North Star.
- Navigate your life's journey with your North Star to guide you.
- Find and successfully pursue opportunities.
- Obtain and maintain a career that is best suited for you.
- Level up in your chosen career field.
- Share your success with those around you.

Ready to live the pathway and create the perfect career trajectory best suited for you?

Let's begin.

Introduction to the Book

The chapters in this textbook are designed to assist you with taking the online course or may be done independently. The course materials contain information that will assist you with knowing your core self. Using that discovery of that core self, you will then understand your "why" — this is the reason for taking the next action steps and following through with what it takes to have the career position best matching all that you are and all that you bring to an employer. After knowing your "Why," the textbook takes you on a pre-career learning journey that prepares you to be a candidate for the career position of your choice.

After you are a successful candidate for a career position and get selected to join your employer in that role, this book takes you on a leveling-up journey sharing tools to enhance your readiness and continuous improvement. It is one thing to get and keep a job, it is quite another to position yourself for leveling up and making a difference in your career field. This is where learning, growing, and developing in your career field makes contributing with compensation even more fun!

Finally, this book takes you on a "lifelong learning" journey in that there is always news to share regarding the positioning for leveling up in your personal and professional lives. In essence, the authors and their organization, Future Forward Academy, have the finger on the pulse. When the pulse changes, you will be aware of what is happening and ready to adapt to the changes along the path of your life's career trajectory.

How to use this book

Use this book as an instructional guidebook. Each chapter will share information that can be applied directly to your life and circumstances. As you absorb this information through various exercises, you will make discoveries (some perhaps for the first time) that will provide insights and directions helpful when designing your career pathway to success. This book complements the online training modules that can be used simultaneously.

Who can benefit from using this book

Anybody seeking joy and purpose as they pursue their personal and professional journey will gain from this book. People who have been on the pathway of their lives not feeling happy, satisfied, or fulfilled, will also benefit from this book. Newly graduated high school or GED people starting on the pathway of life will want to learn and do the lessons in this book to avoid being one of those people not happy, satisfied, or fulfilled in their lives, looking back after 20, 30, 40 or more years and asking what happened. Or—someone caught in this shift taking place in the job market with the machines mixing with humans in the workforce will also benefit.

Job landscape

By 2025, new jobs will emerge and others will be displaced by a shift in the division of labour between humans and machines, affecting:

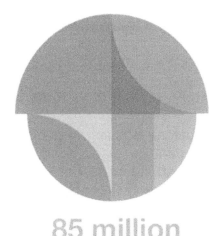

97 million

Growing job demand:
1. Data Analysts and Scientists
2. AI and Machine Learning Specialists
3. Big Data Specialists
4. Digital Marketing and Strategy Specialists
5. Process Automation Specialists
6. Business Development Professionals
7. Digital Transformation Specialists
8. Information Security Analysts
9. Software and Applications Developers
10. Internet of Things Specialists

85 million

Decreasing job demand:
1. Data Entry Clerks
2. Administrative and Executive Secretaries
3. Accounting, Bookkeeping and Payroll Clerks
4. Accountants and Auditors
5. Assembly and Factory Workers
6. Business Services and Administration Managers
7. Client Information and Customer Service Workers
8. General and Operations Managers
9. Mechanics and Machinery Repairers
10. Material-Recording and Stock-Keeping Clerks

Source: Future of Jobs Report 2020. World Economic Forum

TL;DR - AI ChatBot/ChatGPT Questions with AI-generated responses:

The Question:
Q: When will 25% unemployment due to AI occur?
The AI Response:
It is impossible to accurately predict when 25% unemployment due to AI might occur since AI is a rapidly evolving technology. It is possible that this could happen in the future, but it is difficult to estimate a timeline.

Q: Why is AI evolving?

AI is evolving because of the increasing availability of data and computing power. AI technology is continually being improved through machine learning algorithms and data mining techniques, which allow it to better process and analyze data. AI is also becoming more powerful due to advancements in hardware and software technologies.

Q: What jobs will AI replace?
AI will likely replace jobs that are repetitive and involve simple tasks such as data entry, customer service, and certain manufacturing jobs. AI will also be used in more complex roles, such as medical diagnosis and legal research. AI is also likely to replace some jobs that require more advanced skills such as financial analysis and software engineering.

Q: Will AI ever replace educators teaching in K-12 or Higher Education?
No, AI is not likely to replace educators teaching in K-12 or higher education. AI technology can be used to assist teachers in providing personalized learning experiences and can help automate administrative tasks, but AI is not capable of replacing the unique skills and human connection that an educator provides.

This book gives you the tools, all in one place, that you need to begin your pathway or pivot your direction, depending on your situation and circumstance, leading to your success. By the end of this book, you will have everything it takes to get, keep, and level up in the career job position that best matches the true YOU.

SUMMARY OF CONTENTS

Chapter 1: Determine Your "Why"

Begin with the End in Mind (Second Habit from "Seven Habits of Highly Effective People" by Stephen Covey") & Simon Sinek's Golden Circle.

Chapter 2: Determine Your "What"

Your purpose and passion and SMART goal setting.

Chapter 3: Distinguish Yourself-Personal Branding

What makes you special?

Chapter 4: Your LinkedIn Profile

Your link to future career growth and success.

Chapter 5: Other Social Media

I am who the web thinks I am.

Chapter 6: Why You Need Multiple [Paid] Internships

Experience gets you hired - discover what you like and don't like.

Chapter 7: Determine the WHERE to Seek Opportunities

Researching and finding organizations/companies/industries that fit YOU.

Chapter 8: Seeking, Finding, Applying

Where do I go?

Chapter 9: Resume Template

Customization is king and queen.

Chapter 10: The Cover Letter

Do I need one?

1 DETERMINE YOUR "WHY"

*Begin with the End in Mind (*Second Habit from *"Seven Habits of Highly Effective People"* by Stephen Covey") & Simon Sinek's *Golden Circle.*

"People who are crazy enough to think they can change the world are the ones who do."   Steve Jobs, Co-Founder of Apple Computer Inc.,

What this chapter covers:

People gain an understanding of the importance of being prepared to know the steps and have the skills for job prep, job acquisition, job retention, and job advancement to grow in their chosen career fields.

- Appreciate the difference between a job and a career.
- Converting past and current experiences/education into a lifetime loved career.
- Following your passion (do you know what your passion is?).
- Would you like to "love" Mondays, Tuesdays, and Wednesdays...?
- What's YOUR mindset?

In recent years, we went from THE GREAT RESIGNATION to the GREAT RESHUFFLE, along with QUIET QUITTING, to the GREAT REMORSE, to the GREAT REIMAGINATION between 2020 to 2023. This is likely to lead to the GREAT RETRAINING as the turmoil settles down and employers want to retain the employees they have invested so much to find. Emphasis on helping their employees pursue interests and options along the career path of their choice within (or even outside) the organization is also a likely result. It is up to you to be ready to seize these opportunities as they arise.

What happened to people, and the workforce, was evolutionary and revolutionary. Why is this important for you to know? Because the masses of people who resigned from their jobs and refused to work sent a message to the world of work. That message was, "We want more from our jobs; we want decent wages, be able to work from where we want to, and to have meaningful work." There were thousands of comments in the Washington Post, New York Times, and L.A. Times as well as numerous blogs and social media posts from people complaining about the amount of pay not meeting the current cost of living and that their managers treated them as objects, not persons.

This started an awakening that the workforce needs to be in positions that matter the most to them and pay wages that make sense with the current rise in what it costs to support a household and make a living. If you are reading this, perhaps you were among those who took a break from working and joined The Great

Resignation. If that is the case, you may also be among those who found their place working in new positions and then became part of The Great Reshuffle. Perhaps you were one of those people who decided that it was time to return to college and finish your education. Or are you among those people now who have exhausted all their savings and have maxed out their credit cards and have no choice but to take whatever job is possible just to cover daily living expenses, and are not happy, satisfied, or fulfilled?

Chapter One is all about getting to understand your core self, no matter if you are someone who joined the millions of people in the Great Resignation, Great Reshuffle, or the Great Remorse. It is time to get to know your core values, attitudes, interests, and aspirations by which it is possible to find yourself after having become your not true self in the world of work. So, if you are ready to take a moment and leave the rat race, or if you are on a positive path with a desire to learn and grow, let's begin the journey of the discovery of YOU.

Start with the "WHY"

Do you know your true passion(s)? If not, let's find out.

>>> (Optional) You can go to the course workbook. Complete the online exercises:

I remember when... this is found in the online course workbook in: Module 1 – Reflections from the Past Self-Assessment

After completing this exercise, you will begin to see **what** it is that "lights you up" inside and makes you "come alive." You will also have additional insights into your personal values. This is especially important so that you do not end up working for a company whose values do not align with yours. Cultural incompatibility can cause friction that can lead to unhappy, dissatisfied, and unfulfilling work.

After this discovery comes the next step in the process. We need to align WHO YOU ARE with WHAT YOU CAN DO, allowing you to love what you do and to do what you love.

This is especially important when aligning your passion and interests with the skills and education needed for your career.

These skills and education are paramount to you landing a career position that matches the real YOU. When that happens, not only do you "love Monday mornings," but you are in a perfect position where you can continue to excel and have fun while doing it. When you perform with excellence, you are more than likely to be noticed (in a good way), offered additional opportunities to grow, and not only are you likely to stay in the position, but you are most likely to "level up" in your career!!!

Most of the current career education curriculum today focuses on the steps to GET a job. This chapter and the following chapters teach and train you to GET, KEEP, AND LEVEL UP in YOUR CAREER.

This book emphasizes GETTING, KEEPING, and LEVELING UP in your chosen CAREER POSITION. Notice we are not using the word "job." J-O-B has earned the negative connotation of being something that must be done to pay the bills. The organization coordinating the curriculum for this book, Future Forward Academy, focuses on making it possible for you to be placed in a position where you are CONTRIBUTING WITH COMPENSATION. Notice the word "with" and not "for" compensation. If you are contributing with compensation, you are doing what you love, loving what you do, and getting paid for it. The opposite of that is doing what you must do to contribute for which you are paid. As you read this, you can just feel the difference. Which do YOU prefer?

When you are placed in a CAREER POSITION that perfectly aligns with YOU and everything about YOU, there is more likely a different relationship building than if you were in a non-career position. Relationship building in a career position leads to many enjoyable experiences and eventual leveling up. This is the main reason why Future Forward Academy exists; to lead and guide you through the pathway to your career position(s) as you grow and develop professionally and personally. We are, in essence, "clearing the way to make your career pathway" enjoyable and extremely successful offering a lifetime of rewards.

Is it a job or a career? This is a very important question. Many, if not most people, are working a job and not a career. These are the ones who had to be employed with whatever is available and acceptable to pay the bills. There is nothing wrong with this, except it is normally not a path for long-term enjoyment or success.

4

There is much to be said for when you are working and enjoying it, versus not enjoying it.

One of Zig Ziglar's famous quotes is, "*It is your attitude, more than your aptitude, that will determine your altitude*." Simply put, the more you enjoy what you are doing, the more positive your attitude will be. The more positive your attitude, the more those around you will recognize you and your contributions, making it more likely you will move up in your career! This is all the more reason for knowing why you gravitate toward certain activities and why they "light you up" on the inside.

Your mindset is part of the navigation and your compass when traversing your career pathway using your north star as guidance. As you begin and continue your career path, keeping a positive attitude constantly and continually makes a BIT difference. For you to always be positive toward your life and career, knowing and keeping in mind the WHY of what you are doing is extremely helpful. It is like having your own GPS guiding you to your CAREER destination in the same way you would use a GPS to guide you to an address. Your personal and professional GPS is guided mostly by your values. Your values determine what is most important to you. So, in addition to reflecting on your past moments of enjoyment, let's take a moment and see what your values are that help explain and give further insight into **why** it is you do what you do.

>>> (Optional) You can go to the online course workbook and take the values assessment. ---this is part of the online course – Module 1 Values-Based Self-Assessment

After completing the Values Assessment, you are starting to learn more about "what and why" you do the things and enjoy them. This is so very important when determining the best career pathway for you to enjoy and always "love Monday mornings." (Assuming you start your work week on Mondays)

With the combination of the "What" and "Why" insight, you are ready for what comes next in the process. Determining WHAT CAN I DO WITH MY PASSIONS and how those feed into your PURPOSE.

Chapter Summary

- Discovering what lights you up is your passion.
- Your values drive your attitudes and behaviors.
- Your passion feeds your purpose.

TL;DR AI ChatBot/ChatGPT Question:

The Question:
Q: How do I best discover my career passion?

The AI Response:
1. Take a career assessment: Many organizations offer career assessments that can help you identify potential career paths that align with your interests and skills.
2. Explore different industries: It's important to get an understanding of different industries and the roles they offer. Take the time to research and explore different industries, and talk to people in the field to better understand their job roles and responsibilities.
3. Consider your skills and interests: Think about what skills you have and what you're interested in. What kind of work do you find engaging and enjoyable? What do you find yourself naturally gravitating towards?
4. Make a list of dream jobs: Brainstorm a list of dream jobs that you think would make you happy. This is a great way to get an understanding of what you may be passionate about.
5. Experiment and get experience: Once you have a few potential career paths in mind, it's time to get some experience. Look for volunteer and internship opportunities to gain more insight and experience in different roles.
6. Follow your curiosity: Don't be afraid to explore different paths and follow your curiosity. You never know what kind of career opportunities may open up.

Author's Comment on AI Response:
Appropriate suggestions. Career assessment resources, including URL links, are included in the next chapter and can also be found in the ChatGPT conversation in Chapter 17. Key to your success is finding your passion. As they say, "Do what you love and never work a day in your life". You also want to gain a variety of experiences, which is why the authors recommend at least two (paid) Internships for people, and active engagement, including

volunteering at nonprofits/NGOs to gain insights and perspectives.

2 DETERMINE YOUR "WHAT"

Your purpose and passion.

"Kites rise highest against the wind, not with it."
Winston Churchill

Chapter 1 helps to discover the why and what of your passion. Chapter 2 takes that a bit deeper to discover your purpose.

What this chapter covers:

- How passion and purpose are interdependent and provide guidance and direction.
- How to follow your purpose into a career choice.
- How to match values with passion with purpose in creating a career pathway.
- Knowing why and what lights you up make working enjoyable, adding high positive energy to your work and life.
- Being in a job position to contribute **with** (not for) **compensation.**

Have you ever dreamed of a day when someone asks you, "When do you plan to retire?" Some of you smiled when you read this question, and some of you felt eager for that day. What if I were to tell you that you could not only smile at that question but laugh at it too? Why laugh? Because if you are doing what you love to do and loving what you do — there is no need to leave it through retirement.

Many people look at me funny when I answer this retirement plan question with "Retire from what? I am not working! That is a true statement when you are legitimately in a career position where you are enjoying yourself. Why would anyone want to leave such a position where they are fulfilling their purpose and living out their passions? How would you also like to fulfill your purpose and live out your passions? Stay tuned.

There is a process in making it possible for you to be in a career position where you can get to enjoy yourself as you contribute with compensation. You have already completed the first step in the process, which is understanding why and what it is that lights you up inside. Now, we take that a step further by teaching and training you how to align your career path with your values and passions.

YOUR PURPOSE is only sometimes obvious. Many people ask the question, "Why am I here?" This question gets asked at times of moments when it does not look like things are going in the right direction. When it feels hopeless, you won't be able to truly enjoy life.

Passion is all about emotion, and purpose is the focus of passion. This means that now you know what and why you are passionate about certain things, the next step is to focus on that and create a purpose. For example, if someone really enjoys cooking, they might consider their purpose to be making people happy by cooking great meals. Another example might be if someone really lights up inside when they can tell what makes something work electrically; they may have a purpose that includes making things useful for people to have better lives.

Whatever your passion, you can create a purpose.

Marcel Schwantes, from INC.com, put it succinctly, "your passion and purpose are something you can't help yourself with; you must do it, and 'if you weren't getting paid, you would do it anyway' — the purpose is "passionate pursuit". [1]

You see mission, vision, purpose, and core values statements on the websites of companies and organizations all the time. Do you know that those are the means for their compass, giving them direction and guiding them to their "north star?" Without knowing your north star, you can be all over the place, just drifting. Is that what's happening to you now? Are you just drifting in life?

If you are among the millions of people just drifting in life, and you want to have more direction, then you are in the right place as you read this. If you are confident in your purpose, you can reinforce it to maintain your course and direction. For those not sure, you are about to stop drifting and have a direction that gets you to your north star.

The best way to see your purpose from knowing your passion is to take a moment and think. Think about someone watching your life, like in a movie, and they are waiting to see how you are fulfilling what lights you up. How do you see yourself fulfilling what lights you up? Now put that in a way that shows focus. What most people do is create a vision and mission statement. The vision statement paints a picture of what it looks like to fulfill your passion, and the mission statement is what you do to fulfill it, the actions taken fulfilling your vision.

J.D. Roth cautions us to make sure we are true to our passions when creating our purpose in life. For example, some people state their mission is to be debt-free and financially independent. That is their sole purpose in life. But as was pointed out, that is not being true to their true selves and end up being back into debt. [2] Be true to your true self as you create your purpose, aligning it with your passion.

You want to be sure and see what your vision and mission are in life because this affects your time spent with your employer, family, friends, and other activities, along with the time you are away from your employer. Your happiness, enjoyment, and fulfillment are only partially done by contributing with compensation to your employer. And the level of happiness, fulfillment, and joy you have all the time affects the level of your satisfaction with life. So, be honest as you create your own vision and mission statement.

>>> (Optional) You can go to the online course workbook. and complete the exercise: Personal Vision and Mission Statement. This is part of online course Module 2, Your Personal Vision, and Mission Statement Exercise.

Now that you have focused on your passion and described your purpose in a vision and mission statement, you have a compass to guide you to your career north star. It is time for you to match this with a career field.

---

[1]https://www.inc.com/marcel-schwantes/five-simple-exercises-to-find-your-life-purpose.html

[2]https://www.getrichslowly.org/finding-purpose/

CAREER ALIGNMENT

There are many different online software tools to explore what careers fit best with your passion and purpose.

>(Optional) You can go to the online course workbook. and take the O'Net. This is part of the Module 1 Career Assessment Exercise

O'NET is one of the best and fastest ways to see what career fields match the best for you, your true YOU.
https://www.onetonline.org/
The results of this career assessment tool are more direction and guidance for helping you find a career position you enjoy that fulfills

your passion and purpose. Your enjoyment leads to a high level of energy and a high level of positivity. That means when challenges arise with your employer; positivity overrides the situation and circumstances. Positivity drives attitude; as was previously said, attitude drives the altitude by which you reach your employer. Facing challenges with positivity and direction allows for tense periods to pass and for clear and creative thinking to occur. Clear and creative thinking (ethically) is what helps ease the situation and offers feasible (and ethical) solutions. In this way, challenging situations are resolved, and all is well.

There are many life-challenging situations and circumstances too. Having a clear direction along your career pathway is needed. The list of careers best suited to the real YOU may seem overwhelming. It is suggested that you write down the top 5 career fields you discover and start researching them. Here is what you are needing to know as you research each of these career fields:

1. What does it look like to be contributing with compensation in this particular career position? What are the daily duties and responsibilities? Will I enjoy accomplishing the tasks associated with the daily duties and have no problem with fulfilling my responsibilities?
2. What training, experience, or education is needed for this career position? Do I need to gain more training, experience, or education to be successful in this career field?
3. What are some of the employers who hire for this career position?
4. Who are some people I can reach out to and discuss career directions and options (possibly alumni from your institution, family members, or friends of family members)
5. What are the teams like at these employers? What skills or expertise do these teams have that I have too or may be lacking?

These are the questions that need to be answered as you go through the list of O'Net recommended career fields. After researching these career fields, you are ready for the next step in the process.

Choosing a career that fits with your passion and purpose is a challenge given that we are in a new error in the evolution of the workforce. Look below at some of the careers being affected by the advent of mixing humans and AI in the workforce. Many jobs will eventually be done almost entirely by AI. Humans are projected to be replaced in below:

Occupation	Number of Workers
Transportation	3,628,000
Retail salespersons	3,286,000
First line supervisors	3,132,000
Cashiers	3,109,000
Secretaries	3,082,000
Managers, all other	2,898,000
Sales representatives	2,865,000
Registered nurses	2,843,000
Elementary school teachers	2,813,000
Janitors / cleaners	2,186,000
Waiters and waitresses	2,067,000
Cooks	1,951,000
Nursing, psychiatric, and	1,928,000
Customer service	1,896,000
Laborers and freight	1,700,000
Accountants and auditors	1,646,000
First line supervisors	1,507,000
Chief executives	1,505,000
Stock clerks and order fillers	1,456,000
Maids and housekeeping	1,407,000
Postsecondary teachers	1,300,000

Bookkeeping	1,297,000
Receptionists	1,281,000
Construction laborers	1,267,000
Child care workers	1,247,000
Carpenters	1,242,000
Secondary school teachers	1,221,000
Grounds maintenance	1,195,000
Financial managers	1,141,000
Non retail managers	1,131,000

BY 2025, 45% of the working population will be "unemployed through no fault of their own."

This is a partial list. To see the whole list, watch "Humans Need Not Apply" https://www.youtube.com/watch?v=7Pq-S557XQU

Take heart, though job losses to AI, as previously discussed, are projected to be 85 million. It is worth repeating here that it is projected that 97 million will be gained, a net gain of 12 million.

Those additional opportunities will enhance or challenge different skills. Will you be ready? Here is one projection, provided by the World Economic Forum, exploring some of these changes:

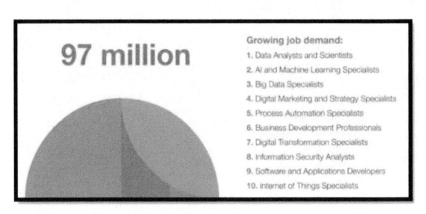

97 million

Growing job demand:
1. Data Analysts and Scientists
2. AI and Machine Learning Specialists
3. Big Data Specialists
4. Digital Marketing and Strategy Specialists
5. Process Automation Specialists
6. Business Development Professionals
7. Digital Transformation Specialists
8. Information Security Analysts
9. Software and Applications Developers
10. Internet of Things Specialists

The key is to find which of these careers in demand best match

14

who YOU ARE and get busy preparing for them.

Chapter Summary

- Your purpose is the action by which your passion is fulfilled.
- There is a way to align your passion and purpose to a career field best suited to your true self.
- Researching the career fields ensures you are placed in a career position you enjoy and thrive.

TL;DR AI ChatBot/ChatGPT Question:

Q: How does one find purpose and passion in their career pursuits?

The AI Response:

1. Identify Your Strengths and Interests: Take some time to reflect on what you're good at and what interests you. Think about what comes naturally to you, the topics you find yourself drawn to, and the activities that you're passionate about.

2. Consider Your Values: Think about what matters to you and what kind of lifestyle you want to lead. This can help you identify a career that aligns with your values.

3. Research Different Fields: Once you have identified your strengths and interests, do some research on different career paths. Research job descriptions, educational requirements, potential salaries, and any other factors that are important to you.

4. Take Action: Once you have identified a career path that aligns with your interests, values, and goals, take action to make it happen. This could mean applying for jobs, signing up for classes, or joining professional organizations.

5. Refine Your Goals: As you gain hands-on experience in your chosen field, you may find that your goals and interests evolve. Be open to exploring different opportunities and adjusting your plans as needed.

Author's Comment on AI Response:

A reasonable summary of the flow to find your purpose and passion. Bottom line, you need to do your homework in exploring areas of interest. You then need to EXECUTE. Nothing gets done unless you act on your findings, actively set goals, and pursue opportunities. Establishing your personal brand starts with knowing what you want and then sharing with the world your why.

3 DISTINGUISH YOURSELF-
PERSONAL BRANDING

What makes you special?

"Be who you are and say what you feel because those who mind don't matter and those who matter don't mind."
Dr. Seuss

As you research the careers by which you are matched at O'Net and discover the details about these careers, you start formulating in your mind how you truly align with these career fields and what you bring to the potential employer.

Assuming you have met the career training, experience, and education requirement, the next thing to think about is how you present yourself to the potential employer seeking to hire someone like you.

What this chapter covers:

- What's your story --" Tell me about yourself."
- What are you proud of? What would you change if given the chance?
- Develop a STRATEGY - What's YOURS?
- What is YOUR Value, Contributions, Accomplishments, and Lessons Learned (what do you bring to the table)/Differentiators - What makes YOU different?
- Time to brag with Metrics - what you have accomplished quantifying the impact of what you have done. How you contributed.
- Awards, unique activities, volunteer efforts, class projects, team involvements, initiatives are taken, leadership roles and recognitions >>>Celebrate your victories.
- Deeper dive into your successes...and what you were THINKING/Attitude when you succeeded. Visualize your success!

Seeking employment does not begin and end with seeking and applying to a job posting, especially when you want to join a team where you contribute with compensation. First, you must believe in your specialty! YOU ARE SPECIAL AND UNIQUE! Now, smile as you nod to this statement.

Next, take this belief into action.
>>> (Optional) You can go to the online course workbook. workbook. This is part of the online course exercise in Module 3: Tell Me About Yourself

Now that you have a three-stage outline of yourself that has captured your attention and energy from the time you were a youngster growing up, you can see your uniqueness and specialness in this world for yourself. You should be proud to share and leverage this as you start your career pathway to success. This is also how you answer the inevitable question, "Tell me about yourself."

You know that in a social setting, meeting someone for the first time, there is a curiosity about the other person that usually starts to get met by asking personal questions. Two people meet up for a blind date, and the uneasiness is lifted when they begin sharing something of themselves with the other person. That same uneasiness is felt by the person or persons tasked with selecting the new team member for the employer. So, the moment you start sharing yourself with them, that uneasiness lifts and a rapport starts to take place.

Now that you have your unique and special story to tell, you can eagerly look forward to it when someone asks you to tell them about yourself. You can look them in the eye and, with confidence, tell them how you are unique and what makes you special and the one they are looking for to join their team.

Developing your strategy

Strategy, putting it simply, is a plan. In this case, the plan is for what you say and what you do as a candidate for a career position. To be effective in executing this plan, you need to prepare.

The Roman philosopher Seneca is credited with saying "Luck is what happens when preparation meets opportunity" (the ancient Romans actually spoke Latin, so this is likely a translation). Time to enhance your luck by being prepared. You already know what to say when someone prompts you to "tell me about yourself." Now, you need to strategize for leveraging what you know.

The best way to plan for what to say about what you know is to prepare and practice. You might have heard of the S-T-A-R method when relating your accomplishments to an interviewer. The acronym stands for:

S - Situation
T - Task at the time
A - Actions that were taken in response to the situation and task
R - Result of the actions that were taken

We are going to modify the S-T-A-R method slightly to reflect a little more efficient technique, known as the C-A-R method which takes a more active tone. It stands for:

C - **Challenge** you were confronted with
A - **Action** you took to solve the challenge
R - **Result** and impact of your actions

We cannot emphasize enough the power of storytelling in an interview or even a conversation. Storytelling engages the listener and allows them to share in the experience and feel what you are talking about, making more memorable the experience you are talking about. The more an interviewer can be inspired by your story, the more top of mind you will appear when they are finalizing decisions on who to hire.

Ideally, you want to have at least three C-A-R examples of challenges you experienced and how you positively and/or creatively generated results that resolved the challenge.

Example: Someone applying to manage a team in a retail store. In the interview, the interviewers ask about a time when they handled a disgruntled customer.

C - Challenge: Frustrated customer called in after receiving the wrong size from an online purchase

A - Actions: Listened calmly to a customer's complaint, empathized with their situation in a reassuring tone, reassured them that we will resolve to their satisfaction, then granted credit to their credit card and invited them to shop online or in the store with a 25% savings coupon.

R - Result: The customer left smiling and ordered multiple additional items in the store — we saved a customer and generated additional loyalty and business!

Creating your CAR means diving deeper into your successes...and what you were THINKING/Attitude when you succeeded. Visualize and fully describe your success with your CAR.

Obviously, a person will have plenty of CARs to share. This is where it can get tricky.

You will need to read the job description for the job posting and research the company to learn about its mission, vision, goals, objectives, and core values. Then, you can better anticipate the interview questions and how it will be possible to insert an appropriate CAR as it applies to their mission, vision, goals, objectives, and core values, as well as the relationship to the duties and responsibilities of the career position.

Having your own CARs to share YOUR Value, Contributions, Accomplishments, and Lessons Learned (what you bring to the table) will demonstrate your effectiveness and create a favorable impression as to what you can accomplish once hired.

>>> (Optional) You can go to the online course workbook. and complete the exercise: The CAR exercise. This is part of an online course Module 3 working in the digital workbook.

Your CARs are also your Differentiators - What makes YOU different?

If there are two people left to be chosen for the one career position slot, how do you show up as different from the other candidate? Simple, your story and your CARs.

BRAG with METRICS

There is a place for bragging about your accomplishments on the resume, and that will be covered in another chapter. In making your strategy for how you show up as a career position candidate, you will need to make a list that includes metrics, and specific numbers that quantify the results of your actions.

The potential employer wants to get an idea of the measure of your future contribution to their team, so they need to know past accomplishments in metrics. Make sense?

For example, someone interviewing for a sales position for an insurance company might want to espouse that they consistently achieved an average of 88% of their sales goals for the 1.5 years they worked as a year-round intern for ABC Insurance Company.

Or, for someone interviewing as a recruiter for a specific industry, that person can brag that every month, without fail, they recruited over 99% of their assigned positions the entire 5 years working for the agency.

Can you begin to see how you can brag with metrics? You are, in essence, celebrating your success and victories in the presence of your interviewer. This is a special moment in which you share your true self and the amount of effort and energy you pour into something you are passionate about. You are also showcasing your talents, gifts, and positivity.

If you are in college with little experience but have played sports, you can brag about how you led your team to victory with specific examples of helping your team improve. You can say, "As a captain on my team, I helped my team win 20% more games in my junior and senior years than they had averaged over the past 20 years (this shows you are an effective team leader).

If you are just out of high school and did not lead a team, but you contributed to the community as a volunteer, that counts too. You can say, "While I was in high school, I volunteered 20 hours each week to tutor and mentor K-6 people at the local community center (this shows you are community minded and giving of your time, talent, and energy).

Making a list of metrics with accomplishments can include awards, unique activities, volunteer efforts, class projects, team involvements, initiatives taken, leadership roles, and recognitions. They all count and can show the interviewers how much they can contribute when you join their team!

>>> (Optional) You can go to the online course workbook. and complete the exercise: How Do You Measure Up? This is part of the online course Module 3 How do you measure up? Your job performance metrics.

Now that you have your list of accomplishments with metrics, you are ready for what comes next.

Celebrate accomplishments

The awards you won, initiatives taken, and their outcomes are examples of acknowledging and celebrating your accomplishments. They are unique activities that speak volumes of who you are as a person and the skills you have acquired.

Class projects while in high school and college count too. They show initiative and drive, which are two major components of innovation. A company thrives when its employees have and apply innovative skills. It also demonstrates team membership experience, and if you led that team, it also demonstrates your leadership skills.

22

In case you are not convinced that this celebration has any value to your job seeking, we invite you to see this list of career skills employers want their employees to possess as found in a survey prepared by NACE (National Association of Colleges and Employers):

ATTRIBUTE	% OF RESPONDENTS SEEKING FOR CLASS OF 2022	% OF RESPONDENTS SEEKING FOR CLASS OF 2021
Problem-solving skills	85.5%	79.0%
Analytical/quantitative skills	78.6%	76.1%
Ability to work in a team	76.3%	81.0%
Communication skills (written)	73.3%	72.7%
Initiative	72.5%	67.8%
Strong work ethic	71.0%	65.4%
Technical skills	64.9%	67.8%
Flexibility/adaptability	63.4%	65.9%
Detail-oriented	62.6%	56.1%
Leadership	60.3%	67.8%
Communication skills (verbal)	58.8%	73.2%
Interpersonal skills (relates well to others)	56.5%	57.6%

Can you now appreciate why celebrating your accomplishments acts as a means for your employer to see your skills and get a taste of the potential value you bring to their team?

Perseverance demonstrated

Taking a deeper dive into demonstrating these accomplishments, you can appreciate the attitude and fortitude it takes to go from concept to completion. Marcel Schwantes, Contributor for Inc.com, says 8% of people actually accomplish their goals.[1] According to the blog: Project Management Statistics: Trends and Common Mistakes in 2022, 70% of projects go uncompleted.[2] If company projects never make it to the finish line, money and time are lost. When they see a job seeker with a track record of accomplishments, they see someone who will work on a team and get things done.

Someone who demonstrates perseverance also demonstrates sticktoitiveness, focus, attention, and attentiveness, someone who has what it takes to get the job done and done well. If an employer is seeking someone like you, why wouldn't they be eager to meet you and schedule an interview?

[1] Science Says Only 8 Percent of People Actually Achieve Their Goals. Here Are 7 Things They Do Differently | Inc.com

[2] https://teamstage.io/project-management-statistics/

Chapter summary

- You need to know and appreciate your self-worth and the value you bring to an employer.
- See all that you have accomplished and be proud to share this with a potential employer.
- Develop the strategy and stories that best fit your uniqueness, capabilities, and career path.
- See, share, and celebrate your achievements because they demonstrate your character and characteristics that attract your employer to you.

TL;DR AI ChatBot/ChatGPT Question:

The Question:
How do I best develop soft skills?

The AI Response:
1. Practice active listening.
2. Take on responsibilities outside of your comfort zone.
3. Work on communication and presentation skills.

4. Take part in team-building activities.
5. Develop empathy and understanding of others.
6. Develop problem-solving and critical thinking skills.
7. Develop positive self-talk.
8. Be adaptable and open to change.
9. Develop your self-awareness.
10. Take time to practice self-care.

Author's Comment on AI Response:

Soft Skills, what I prefer to call Success Skills (nothing soft about them!), are key to succeeding along your chosen path. Developing these skills will aid you in your personal and professional journey so that you will be ready and able to take advantage of opportunities as they come your way. And with these skills, more opportunities WILL come your way! An organization worth exploring that covers a majority of the ChatGPT attributes listed is www.Toastmasters.org. Don't forget, the journey is the reward. You also want your LinkedIn profile and resume, as it reflects your personal brand, to demonstrate your active engagement and successes in pursuing your growth and development.

4 YOUR LINKEDIN PROFILE

Your link to future career growth and success.

"If you want to go somewhere, it is best to find someone who has already been there."
Robert Kiyosaki, Coauthor *Rich Dad Poor Dad*

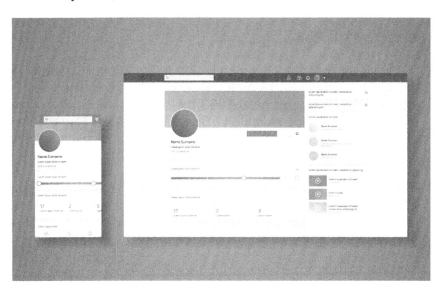

What this chapter covers:

- Presenting your brand.
- You're in sales (introduce Canva).
- 5-7 seconds (opinion machine starts running).
- Keywords

- Complete all sections.
- Growing your network.
- Prepare your Basic Profile on LinkedIn.
- Have someone look at your profile and give feedback.
- Ethical considerations.

Now that you know your unique story, your passion, and your purpose, and can sense your specialness, it is time to put this all together digitally. This is a digital representation of *YOUR* uniqueness, accomplishment, life goals, and interests, as well as your passion and purpose in life.

The LinkedIn Profile is where over 90% of human resource professionals go to learn about a candidate's fit for the position. In the case of a career position, this fit must be airtight. So, that means your LinkedIn profile must be an accurate representation of YOUR TRUE SELF!

PUTTING YOUR BEST FOOT FORWARD: PRESENTING YOUR BRAND.

By the Numbers

Over half of the approximately 900 million global LinkedIn users in over 200 countries are on the mobile platform, so you want to be mobile aware. Approximately 260 million U.S. adults are currently on board - that's approximately 75% of U.S. adults. That means the platform is pretty popular. Half of these users are on at least once a month, with many actively participating daily. The male-female split is about 57% male/43% female. 45% of U.S. users are in upper management. Another key figure is that it is estimated that over 90% of recruiters and human resource folks use it as they search for interview candidates. It also doesn't hurt that 41% of millionaires also use LinkedIn. Take full advantage of your access to this network.

It's Your Career

As a career position candidate, you have a lot to offer, and this is what you need to showcase in your LinkedIn profile. You show who you are, what you have done, what skills you possess, where you have contributed, how you have learned and grown, and how you are poised to continue learning, growing, and contributing. This showcasing becomes YOUR BRAND.

If you don't share and brag (sometimes gently, sometimes aggressively) about your accomplishments, who will? Now is not the time to be modest. Readers want to hear YOUR STORY. Like the resume, which will be covered in a later section, your LinkedIn profile tells your story. But you need to impress your audience quickly. Both LinkedIn profiles and resumes need to capture the reader's attention in the first 5-7 seconds. The added benefit is that LinkedIn allows you to enter keywords that get you found without having to blast resumes around the globe. Many professionals say they prefer LinkedIn over the resume because of its accessibility and flexibility.

How do I stop the press and impress the reader with my profile and get found? Just like meeting somebody for the first time, your initial impression is crucial. The following items need to be at their best as these are the first things that are seen on your profile. The discussion below is not cast in stone and there are many exceptions to the rules. These foundational thoughts will get you kicked off in the right direction. It starts with making your profile searchable, and then when you are found, drawing in the viewer. If that sounds like storytelling to you, it is!

What does a viewer see initially when accessing my profile? Visually, your picture and background banner are the starting point. Then your name and headline, mostly text, reinforces that first impression. The About sections give you more space than your headline to discuss what benefits an employer will gain if/when they hire you. The key to remember is that your profile is NOT about you, it's about what you can do for your potential employer. What do you bring to the table that will help THEM succeed?

The first rule of using LinkedIn is to commit the time and effort, ideally every day for at least ten minutes, to make it work for you. You also need to understand why you are using LinkedIn. You then want to make your profile inviting and SEARCHABLE through the inclusion of keywords that potential employers will be using to find you. You then proceed and make connections like crazy. Your target is to, in short order, exceed the 500-connection mark. This signals to active professionals that you are a serious LinkedIn user.

So, what is it about having more connections that help people find you? The term 1st-degree connection refers to people that you have invited to connect with, and they have accepted that invitation, or they invited you and you accepted. This gives you many benefits. You can now send InMail messages, LinkedIn's equivalent to email, for free. If you want to send such messages to 2nd-degree connections, defined as 1st-degree connections connected to your 1st degrees which you are not directly connected to, it will cost you.

The bigger advantage is best understood by knowing how LinkedIn conducts its searches. Let's say that a recruiter types in the keywords "Python", "data analytics", and "accounting" to find a potential candidate. LinkedIn will first search through the recruiter's 1st-degree connections, then proceed to search 2nd degrees, and then go beyond to the 3rd-degree connections. This means that if I had this recruiter as a 1st-degree connection and was also connected to you, the recruiter has a better chance at finding you. The recruiter would not be alerted to me because I do not have all those keywords but as a 2nd-degree connection through me, could find you. Here is a picture to help you visualize the relationships.

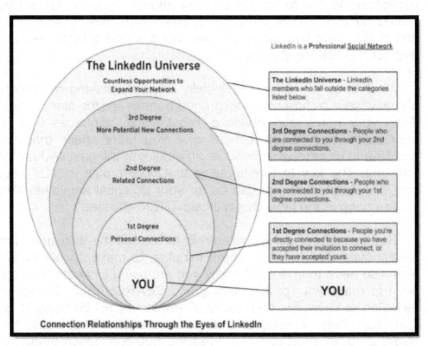

Connection Relationships Through the Eyes of LinkedIn

Hopefully, this helps you understand the value of gaining more 1st degree connections in your network. You might have heard or seen Kevin Bacon's 1993 movie "Six Degrees of Separation" highlighting how our connections can quickly get us to virtually anybody, including the President of the United States. To paraphrase an ancient Chinese proverb about planting a tree, "The best time to start networking was five years ago, the second-best time is now". Let's discuss further some of the specific elements that will make your profile shine.

Barebone Features:

Picture - A picture is worth a thousand words. Your visual image projects your professionalism. Unless you are seeking to be a Harley Davidson mechanic, you probably don't want your HD tee shirt and Live to Ride tattoo on full display. Being in synch with the position you seek is most appropriate. A finance or accounting role would typically be a little dressier while a high-tech role might lean towards being a little more casual. It is typically better to overdress than to underdress which means you most likely don't need a tuxedo but do need to appear clean and professional. You do want a photo of just you, appropriately dressed, well-lit, and SMILING, typically including just your head and shoulders without any background distractions. Many advocates a professional headshot which could be well worth the investment, but recent trends towards showing you as approachable allow for you to use your own camera/phone to take your photo. But do not take it as a selfie or take it while in your car unless you are seeking a NASCAR driver role, and even then, think twice.

Banner - The most underrated and largest piece of screen real estate is your banner. Leaving the default banner unmodified wavy image broadcasts "LinkedIn newbie". You want to take advantage of that large space to draw in your viewer. Using a tool like www.Canva.com allows you to import pictures, create images, and add text. Show off your brand with your banner. You can include a favorite quote, image, award, publication, or just an interesting picture that reflects the environment in which you are seeking to secure an opportunity. School spirit is fine if it is not too busy or distracting. What message do you want to send to a potential employer?

Reflect on that answer and then produce the banner that shows who you are or want to be with the reader.

Headline/Tagline - Highlights your personal brand. This is where typically the most valuable words on the page are found...no pressure. Well okay, a little pressure. We mentioned keywords earlier. Keywords placed in your headline get 3X-5X recognition when someone is searching for the attributes you have. What should be here is NOT the current position you have, but the position you seek. Think about it. Which do you think is the most effective headline: 1. Junior Marketing Major at XYZ University or 2. Cashier at Piggly Wiggly or 3. Aspiring Social Media Marketer Seeking an internship? I hope you selected 3! Your headline should be aspirational, looking toward the future position rather than your present or past position, unless you are seeking the same or similar role.

About Section - Now you can brag, though beware of being braggadocious! You want to make it easily readable and have it tell your story with an emphasis on what you can do for potential employers. You want the tone to be upbeat and positive. It should be in the first person. Visually you want bullets or shorter lines rather than long paragraphs. Such paragraphs tend to make it harder to keep the reader's attention. Always include your contact information, including email, and ideally phone towards the end of the body of this section. You also want to present your story. Accomplishments, achievements, and anything else that you can think of that employer might say "I want this kind of a person working with us. Sounds like they can make a positive difference". You also want to include a recommended CTA (call to action) to let the reader know the next step in reaching out to you should they desire to do so.

Experience Section - Include not only jobs, titles, and timing, but also accomplishments associated with each of the roles you have had. Ideally, you will quantify those accomplishments. This is another area to include keywords as found on job descriptions for the types of roles you are pursuing. Dates must be consistent with your resume. If you have additional experiences that may not be specifically jobs, you can and should include leadership roles in school clubs/organizations as well as volunteer activities in which you made a difference. Sometimes class projects can also be highlighted.

Education Section - Includes the institutions that you have attended. You can even put your high school if you choose. Additional details, such as honors and recognitions should also be included.

Skills Section - Highlight the skills that your potential employers are seeking. You can receive endorsements for those skills from your network. If you go to the **Demonstrate Skills** subsection, you can use the "Take Skills Assessment" to demonstrate your knowledge and ability to use tools such as Excel, Python, and a whole bunch more.

Other Sections - Highlighting licenses, certifications, languages, and volunteer activities will help to round out your profile giving readers a fuller picture of who you are. You also want to get AND give recommendations regularly. Readers not only see the recommendations you get but can also see those you give. LinkedIn makes it easy to request recommendations, but it may not hurt to have some drafts made when you seek a recommendation from someone.

Advanced features to make you shine

There are also some features that you might want to use that can only be initiated from a mobile device. Two examples of these features are the ten-second audio and 30-second video that can be attached to your profile. The audio is typically used for name pronunciation and when someone clicks on the microphone next to your name if you have made a recording, they will hear whatever you record. Instead of name pronunciation, as mine is pretty easy, I added an additional tagline about what I can do for the reader.

You also will want to change your URL name through the settings. Which would you find easier to remember: https://www.linkedin.com/in/scott-dell-994669248/ or https://www.linkedin.com/in/drscottcpa/?

As you will ultimately be placing this on your resume, email signature blocks, presentations, and anywhere else you can, you want it recognizable and easy to remember. This is still part of your branding and messaging, so take full advantage.

>>> (Optional) You can go to the online course workbook. and complete the exercise: Complete the LinkedIn exercise found in Module 4 LinkedIn Assignment

So now it's time for the why and how of LinkedIn networking

So why is it important to network? You heard earlier that over 80% of internships and jobs are found through networking. Having a plurality of 1st-degree connections is advantageous, especially if you want to be found in searches, it's time to connect like a mad dog, assuming mad dogs use LinkedIn. Connect with friends, parents of friends, classmates, colleagues, strangers, exes, professionals, executives, faculty members, and even alumni from your school/s. Remember, everybody knows somebody, and those somebody might be looking to hire you.

To aid in networking and promoting your brand, you also want to be posting. A post is when you share your insights and invite others with similar interests to comment on your post. You can start by reacting and leaving comments on other people's posts. You WILL be noticed. You will also want to join LinkedIn groups in professional and personal interest areas. Once you join these groups and are accepted, you will have instant access to the membership list with whom you may want to reach out and connect.

Note: Make sure to personalize EVERY invite you make so that the potential connection knows why you might want to connect and what your common interests might be. Alumni of your institution are especially easy to gain access to. Would you refuse an invite like *"Hi Sam, I noticed on your profile that you have an amazing and unique financial background! As a current student and fellow Badger would be honored to be added to your LinkedIn professional network!! In appreciation of your consideration, Scott?"*

Most alumni would welcome the opportunity to help an up-and-coming future alum or current colleague from the same institution.

The Informational Interview

One of the most powerful ways to build your exposure and network is to conduct Informational Interviews with people at companies that are doing interesting things that may match your career goals. LinkedIn's alumni feature is one of my personal favorites for making connections. You can see ALL alums, their pictures (if they include one), names, and titles, and ultimately click on them to access their profile.

The purpose of an informational interview is NOT to ask for a job or interview. It is designed to gather information, expand your network, and impress the potential connection while learning about their career path. Once accepted as a connection above, reach out with a message like "Thank you for connecting. I admire the career path that has taken you to where you are today. As a fellow future business professional majoring in finance, I would love to learn more about how you obtained your current role. Would you be open to a 15-minute virtual or live conversation to chat about your successes and challenges? We could set up an appointment at your convenience via https://Calendly.com/DrScottCPA, or you can respond to this request directly to coordinate a time. In appreciation, Scott".

This informational interview is just that, informational. You want to discuss how they got to where they are and the path they followed. Believe me, if they get to know you/like you and are aware of any opportunities, they will volunteer for them - as they often earn cash rewards for referrals within their companies. One of my student's success stories is when he actually listened to this idea and executed it flawlessly. He reached out and set up the interview. After talking for over 45 minutes for what was scheduled for 15 minutes, he was told, ", we have two internship opportunities that we are about to post. You would be ideal for one of those. Are you interested?" Any guesses as to what their answer was?

You are entering an exclusive club of go-getters that are interested in personal and professional growth. Wishing you success on the journey!

Connecting on LinkedIn

When seeking to reach out to a potential connection, you want to make it easy for them to say yes. That does not happen if you are trying to pitch or sell something out of the gate. Once you are clear on your purpose, you want to share commonalities and give them a reason to get to know you. Though it might be possible to build your network by just hitting "Connect" without an introductory message, you lose an opportunity to start the relationship from a mutually beneficial perspective. You may be quite aware that you are seeking a career role when reaching out but asking for such a "favor" on a first contact is a stretch. It is like proposing (or accepting a proposal) for marriage after a three-minute conversation. Typically, this does not give the recipient a good first impression.

Ideally, you will be reaching out to build a relationship and develop rapport. To do this, you need to review their profile and find commonalities (same school, degree, hobbies, interests, or professional affiliations, participated in the same event). You only get 300 characters in the invitation to prove yourself worthy as a potential connection. A sample message might look like this:

Hi Scott,

Enjoyed meeting you at the XYZ event. As a fellow Badger (note: UW mascot) and financial professional, I would be honored to be added to your LinkedIn network. You might also enjoy the Forbes article at www.forbes.com/article.

In appreciation,

Jan

In the above example, you are giving context for where you might have met, the commonality of being part of the same institution, and you have taken the initiative to give before you get - the first rule of networking.

Another example of someone you may never have met, and it is okay to reach out to strangers, might be:

Jordan,
Congratulations on your success as a Big 4 staff auditor. As a current accounting major at your alma mater, I would be honored to connect with you.

Thank you for your consideration,

Alex

As you can see from the above examples, all you are trying to do is briefly share something in common in a positive tone, so they will accept your invitation. Once they accept, you have plenty of space for a longer message as you are not limited to 300 characters as in your original invitation.

Once you have established a connection, looked at their profile, see any posts they may have initiated (and hopefully reacted and commented on those posts), groups they may have joined (possibly joined the same or similar groups), or other activities they have participated in, you can then reach out to further build rapport. You are now ready to perform additional outreach. Again, you are not asking for a job or job referral at this point. Reaching out for an informational interview might be a great next step. Such as:

Bobbi,

Thanks for connecting. It looks like since graduating as a finance major, your career path has been exciting and interesting. As a fellow finance major, would you be available for a brief 15-minute chat to share your successes and challenges? I am graduating in a year and have learned the value of learning from others. Finding out about how your achievement led you to where you are today would mean a lot to me, and I could share additional insights about exciting things happening at your alma mater. Are there any afternoons between 3 and 5 that could work for you if you might be able to spare some time? Please do not feel obligated if your schedule is full, but if you can find the time, I would be in your debt.

Thank you for your consideration,

Pat

By expanding your network on LinkedIn, you become plugged into an environment that professionals regularly engage in to grow their network and careers. Ultimately, it will enhance both for you.

AI ChatBot/ChatGPT Question:

The Question:
How do I put my best foot forward on LinkedIn?

The AI Response:
1. Complete your profile. Make sure all the information is up to date, that your photo is professional, and that you've included your experience and accomplishments.
2. Connect with people in your field and industry. Reach out to colleagues, former employers, and other professionals who could be potential contacts.

3. Participate in groups. Find and join groups related to your industry and engage in conversations by commenting and sharing content.

4. Publish articles. Writing and sharing articles on LinkedIn is a great way to showcase your expertise and increase your visibility.

5. Build your network. Reach out to other professionals to expand your network and increase your chances of being discovered.

6. Optimize your profile. Use relevant keywords in your profile so that you can be found in searches.

7. Follow companies. Follow companies in your industry to stay up to date on news, job postings, and other opportunities.

Author's Comment on AI Response:

Bottom line. To grow your LinkedIn footprint and exposure, you need to ENGAGE. Reach out to colleagues and potential colleagues. Post and publish, starting with commenting on other people's posts will get you noticed. Connect to people that comment on your posts/comments. Reaching out and connecting to group members in your areas of interest, along with alumni from your institution, will go a long way in helping you network and build your base of connections. Don't forget the other social media environments that can get you additional exposure while providing you with valuable insights as you research companies and people.

5 OTHER SOCIAL MEDIA

I am who the web thinks I am.

"Many people are afraid of the dark, but the real tragedy is those who are afraid of the light"
Plato

What this chapter covers:

- The Billboard Effect
- Google yourself.
- Use it to your advantage.
- Which platforms are for YOU?

- Professional versus personal posts

Putting yourself in the limelight for employers to find you is a necessity. We are in a social media-driven society. Think about it for a minute. We get our public and private news from social media. We stay in touch with our friends and family through social media. We learn different ways of doing things via social media, and we are dependent on social media at times for communication with friends and family as well as for entertainment. So, why not market yourself as a viable job candidate and leverage social media to enhance your effectiveness? This is not a "nice to do" but is a "need to do".

Using social media is part of the process of getting noticed by an employer. You want to ensure that what your potential employer sees will attract them to you. To make that happen you need to know what they will see when they seek you out...which they definitely will.

Isabel Thottam, a *Monster* contributor, wrote, "Picture job searching as a two-way mirror. On one side, there's you: a hopeful job seeker Googling everything and anything you can find out about your dream employer. On the other side is your potential employer who can look in every nook and cranny online to learn all about you—including your social media mistakes.[1] " Ouch!

According to Thottam's article, 67% of the time, a potential job candidate is screened using social media. She also said, "21% of employers polled said they wouldn't consider someone who **doesn't** have a social presence. It looks like you either have something to hide or nothing to show, both of which will send your resume to the bottom of the pile."[1]
So, to be in the running with your competition, you need to have a clean social media presence, and the kind of presence employers would be proud to have seen.

So, what can you do?

- Leverage the power of social media.
- Connect to industry leaders, associations, publications, and influencers in your career field.
- Participate in online groups in your career industry. Share and comment on relevant posts and blogs.

- Show the type of contributions you are bringing to the potential employer and how you can add value to their organization and the industry.

Isabelle also said, "When researching candidates, employers review social media channels to determine if the candidate posts smart, funny, insightful, interesting, or creative content. This is your chance to show companies you're the full package and that you're more than your one-dimensional resume." [1] This means paying attention to the field via social media and contributing to the discussion professionally knowing that in the future, what you wrote will matter to someone considering you as their next new team member.

The Billboard Effect

We mention this because it has happened to us. We applied for a specific job using a professional social media environment or resume database like LinkedIn, indeed, Monster, etc. Because our resume was made public, other companies saw it and acted on it. This is like when you are on the internet booking a flight and see an ad for a hotel at your destination and you click on the ad. As a job seeker, you want to be seen and discovered, especially by an employer that may be a perfect match for both you and them!

Just like when a billboard is created and placed on the side of the road for people to see, you need to create a "job-seeking billboard" that projects your branding and image. This is done by having a comprehensive and focused resume consistent with your LinkedIn profile and other social media. These channels need to be aligned with your dream job/role/position.

For example, your passion might be early childhood education. Your purpose is to ensure that children between the ages of 2 and 4 are educated to the extent they are ready to enter school with the foundational basics needed to succeed. Let's say that at the time you are creating this job-seeking billboard, you are a school janitor attending the last two years of college, pursuing an undergraduate degree in education with an emphasis on early childhood education. In this case, you are building a LinkedIn profile showcasing yourself as someone contributing to the lives of children 2-4 years old as a volunteer or part-time employee at a Pre-K facility. You are also reading, sharing, and commenting on posts and blogs about how early childhood education is going well or not doing well. By having your resume accessible and your social media presence active, you are creating a job-seeker billboard by which potential employers can discover you. They are then able to take action to get to know more about you while seeing more of you on social media. They can then take the initiative to reach out and contact you for an interview!

Now you can appreciate why we are introducing you to the Billboard Effect. It is so you are making it more possible for the potential employer to discover you.

Google Yourself

You can likely guess why we want you to "google yourself." This will reveal what the potential employer will see when THEY GOOGLE YOU, and they will. Oh, oh, does this mean you may need to do some fixing to your social media image? Possibly. If so, stay tuned.

Fixing a social media image is not easy, but it is doable. Since we have social media mediums such as Facebook, Twitter, TikTok, LinkedIn, and Instagram, it is possible to place posts that explain and reduce the negative impact of some previous postings. This is how you fix your social media image.

Write posts on the big four social media: LinkedIn, Facebook, Twitter, and Instagram, that counter the posts or sharing that might have occurred at a moment when original high emotions have cooled. It is a human condition, and we all recognize when in the heat of passion, we may say or do something we later regret. If someone can't forgive that moment, they are a hypocrite. So, posting something that speaks to that is showing authenticity and honesty, which are two traits' employers appreciate in their employees. Taking responsibility for your actions and behaviors, along with correcting any ill will created by them, is a sign of maturity and self-awareness.

>>> (Optional) You can go to the online course workbook. and complete the exercise: "Google Yourself" exercise. This is part of the online course Module 5 Other Social Media Assignment.

Use It to your advantage

Leveraging the effectiveness of social media is a great way for you to be discovered and appreciated. Not only can you show what you are contributing to your employer, but you are

According to Thottam's article, 67% of the time, a potential job candidate is screened using social media. She also said, "21% of employers polled said they wouldn't consider someone who **doesn't** have a social presence. It looks like you either have something to hide or nothing to show, both of which will send your resume to the bottom of the pile."[1]

Be conscious of your social media presence. Make sure it's a presence employers would welcome.

So, what can you do?

- Leverage the power of social media.
- Connect to industry leaders, associations, publications, and influencers in your career field.
- Participate in online groups in your career industry. Share and comment on relevant posts and blogs.
- Show the type of contributions you are bringing to the potential employer and how you can add value to their organization and the industry.

Isabelle also said, "When researching candidates, employers review social media channels to determine if the candidate posts smart, funny, insightful, interesting, or creative content. This is your chance to show companies you're the full package and that you're more than your one-dimensional resume." [1] This means paying attention to the field via social media and contributing to the discussion professionally knowing that at some point in the future, what you wrote will matter to someone considering you as their next new team member.

Which platforms are for YOU?

We are all familiar with Facebook, Twitter, LinkedIn, and Instagram, but did you know there are other such platforms that professional industries and associations subscribe to and use as a means of communication? For example, Reddit is an e-magazine and a posting message board used by several different industries in the Arts and Sciences. The Chronicle of Higher Education and

NACE are two places online where educators, employees, and higher education advocates go to share ideas, events, thoughts, news, and a lot of other things that could influence the future of higher education participants.

You want to engage on the platform where your potential employer may be and where your career field experts communicate. [2]

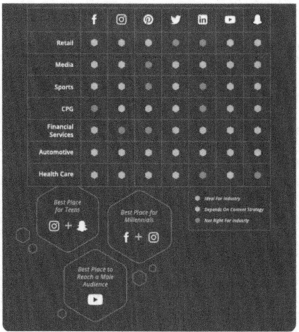

: https://www.socialmediatoday.com/news/Best-Social-Platforms-by-Industry-Infographic/636331/

You will notice that if your career field is retail, you might want to deemphasize your efforts on Twitter and LinkedIn. If your career field was in healthcare, you would want to focus your time and energy on Facebook, Pinterest, and Twitter.

Personal versus professional posting

Needless to say, if you are reporting on the scrumptious meal you and a friend just had on Facebook, that is considered personal posting. If you posted something about the changes in regulation taking place affecting the financial services industry, that is considered professional. Why does this even matter for a book like this one?

The reason why we are emphasizing the difference between these two posts is this: THEY MATTER GREATLY TO SOMEONE LOOKING TO HIRE YOU. What you post on social media is potentially seen by everyone unless you change the privacy settings. You will want to safeguard your personal posts from being seen by people outside your inner circle. This gives you freedom of expression without later regret.

By the same token, you want to be sure and post the best and most valuable insights you can create on the appropriate social media channels where they can be noticed. Make sure to do your homework and check your facts. Do not get caught up in a frenzy that might not be true. For example, there is a political sway taking place on social media and you get caught up in it.

Be careful. When taking a political stance on social media and you are a job candidate, you are playing with fire. If your stance does not match with the employer or is too controversial, they will look for someone else to join their team. Even after researching the company you want to work with and learning their stance on an issue, they may change that stance in the future which makes your stance counterproductive and of no value. So, be very careful what you post politically on social media.

Another rule of thumb that you may have heard or learned from a parent is "If you can't say something nice, don't say anything at all." Take this one to heart. If you rant and rave online with negative content it provides a direct reflection of you and your personality. Employers will think twice, and even three times, about having you join their team. If they thought they had a potentially valuable team member but find them spewing negative comments about people and situations, game over. You do not want to be in that situation.

Social media posting is a way for employers to get to know you, your character, beliefs, and the strengths they are seeking in a candidate. So, give them what they want to see (authentically and ethically). Your LinkedIn profile with endorsements and recommendations helps tremendously, To make these even more effective contributing your thoughts and expertise where and when it is appropriate to do so reinforces your value. This also helps you get noticed, discovered, and respected in your chosen career field.

[1]https://www.monster.com/career-advice/article/these-social-media-mistakes-can-actually-disqualify-you-from-a-job

[2]https://www.socialmediatoday.com/news/Best-Social-Platforms-by-Industry-Infographic/636331/

https://toggl.com/blog/social-media-screening

"You can see why many recruiters love social media—it allows them to discover all the information they aren't allowed to ask about during an interview. But that's a problem, because one of the hallmarks of legal hiring practices is that they focus on behaviors within the work context. There should be a clear distinction between what people do during work and what they do outside of it."

Chad Van Iddekinge, Professor at the University of Iowa | HBR

Chapter Summary

- There is Billboard Effect and ways in which you can create your own jobseeker billboard.
- Your social media presence matters greatly so it behooves you to protect it and present it in the best way possible.

- Leveraging social media channels while seeking a position on a team with an employer you wish to work with is the best possible way to be noticed, discovered, and networked with acknowledgment and appreciation possibly resulting in career employment.

AI ChatBot/ChatGPT Question:

The Question:
What is the best way to leverage social media in my job search?

The AI Response:
1. Create a professional profile on LinkedIn and start networking.
2. Research companies and recruiters on Twitter and connect with them.
3. Post relevant content on your social media channels to demonstrate your expertise.
4. Use hashtags to highlight your skills and experience.
5. Follow relevant companies and industry leaders on Twitter to stay up-to-date on job postings.
6. Reach out to your connections on social media to ask for referrals.
7. Use YouTube and other video platforms to showcase your talents.
8. Join relevant industry groups and participate in conversations.

Author's Comment on AI Response:
Bottom line. Though the AI response appears to be Twitter-heavy, your research can and should include multiple sources of information on the companies you are exploring. Be aware, you can't, and shouldn't, be everywhere. But wherever you are active, be it LinkedIn, Facebook, Instagram, TikTok, Snapchat, or another platform, actively engage on that platform and let folks know who you are, the insights you have to offer, and what you are looking for. Everybody knows somebody! And when you find an internship or job opportunity, let the world know!

6 WHY YOU NEED MULTIPLE [PAID] INTERNSHIPS

Experience gets you hired - discover what you like and don't like.

"Life will give you whatever experience is most helpful for the evolution of your consciousness."
Eckhart Tolle, spiritual teacher

What this chapter covers:

- Why internships are valuable to future careers.
- The different types of internships.
- Finding one or multiple internships.
- Post-internship and getting hired.

Why Internships

I want to get a good job when I graduate. But how do I know if I will be good at it? How do I know if I will even like it? How might I get that extra edge that will put me over the top when competing against others for the same opportunities? If you haven't guessed by now, the answer to all three of those questions can be getting an internship, or better yet, getting multiple internships.

Internships are an ideal way to test the waters of your career choice. Finding out what you like about your potential future field is powerful and can enhance your commitment. Finding out what you don't like can be even more powerful by highlighting the things you can't be passionate about. It might also introduce you to new areas within your chosen field that will get you fired up.

For example, this author, majoring in accounting, managed an H&R Block tax office while an undergraduate student. I realized that I did not have a passion for tax accounting. Not that I didn't like helping others through this potentially confusing process and saving folks money, but I realized that my interest was more about business rather than learning and following tax rules and laws. I might have considered tax preparation more appealing if I was interested in the law. I do have a passion for business and accounting, but finding out while an undergrad that taxes were not my thing thankfully prevented me from graduating and pursuing opportunities that might have had a heavy tax component. I still obtained my CPA and worked for two major accounting firms, but taxes were not the place where my skills, passions, and talents could be best applied.

Besides exploring potential careers, there are a multitude of additional benefits to gaining experience through internships. Participating in a variety of activities will yield a better understanding of the profession and of yourself. You usually cannot really tell if you like something until you get to experience doing it. Once that is accomplished, you will normally either gain further commitment or realize that the activity is not for you. Internships are an opportunity to explore and experience, in a much lower-risk environment than in your first professional role post-graduation.

Through internships and similar work experiences, you will gain professional skills and an understanding of the work environment. You will also gain insights into your capabilities and strengths. By default, this will also boost your confidence knowing that you have been exposed to and succeeded in performing within the field. Additional skills of working in teams, and communicating with peers and colleagues, along with enhanced professional bearing, are additional benefits that you will experience.

The opportunity to network should not be underestimated. You have already heard that over 80% of jobs (and internships) are found through networking. What is a better way to set yourself up for future potential success, and build relationships with potential colleagues that will benefit you far into the future, than to start networking right away? I can't think of one!

Internships are typically easier to obtain than full-time jobs post-graduation. Usually, there are fewer applicants, which enhances the prospects of increasing the odds of obtaining a placement. The bonus is that national statistics indicate that over 50% of people with internships will get job offers directly from those internships. It sure beats being in an applicant pool of 300+ hoping to get that interview and offer from an employer that does not know you.

Paid or Unpaid, Local or Distant - Which Would You Prefer?

Paid internships are the most valuable. NACE (National Association of Colleges and Employers) surveys have revealed that paid internships usually yield higher responsibilities along with better experiences...and a higher potential for getting an offer at the end of it all. If an employer is willing to pay you, they usually expect more productive work out of you and take you more seriously. This also typically leads to better outcomes with more active engagement in the field.

Payment can take many forms. Of course, there is the base wage, but there is also the potential opportunity to gain skills and training for a variety of tools while on the job. In the business world, Tableau (and Microsoft Power BI) is sometimes considered the "new Excel". Upon completion of any business program, you are expected to have solid Excel skills. Even non-businesspeople should have Excel proficiency. If you can gain training and exposure either to advanced Excel opportunities or other software tools, you are way ahead when it comes to your job prospects. You might even discover some tools that you have never even heard of on the job and will get you more excited upon returning to the classroom while applying those skills gained from your internship.

As for travel opportunities, many companies, and even some schools like mine, will help subsidize travel, housing, and other necessities that will help you take advantage of internships located outside of your immediate area. If you can get exposure to another city, state, or country, not only do you get the benefit of the work experience, but you get to see a different living environment that will give you insights into how other people and cultures interact. It may also help you to determine if you might be interested in traveling or relocating after graduation or confirm a desire to stay local. Either way, the experience you gain is valuable personally and professionally. An added benefit is that you have additional interesting experiences to share on your resume and LinkedIn profile, as well as in an interview. I assure you; interviewers would much rather hear about your travel experiences than your GPA!

Finding One or Multiple Internships

Competition for many internships may be less rigorous than for full-time job postings. Some of the larger companies will attract a high number of applications though they also often have a larger number of internship positions available. Be warned: Many of the Fortune 500 companies looking for a summer intern will open the application process at the end of August of the previous year and close applications by September! This means if you start looking in the spring, your chances are almost zero for getting into these companies.

Similar to the trend in job hunting, internship hunting is also best accomplished by targeting a specific company rather than just a job or major title. Job boards can be a potential lead source but should not be your only source. Networking and focused energy in pursuing specific organizations and opportunities will yield the greatest success. The 80% figure of jobs and internships being found through networking, as previously mentioned, are real!

The informational interview, especially using the alumni feature as mentioned in the LinkedIn chapter, is one of the best ways to gain an understanding of your field and pursue opportunities. Remember, during this "interview", virtual or live, you are seeking information about career paths and organizations, not asking for a job from the interviewer. The person that you get to talk to will often take the initiative of suggesting opportunities in their company if they find you interesting and potentially a good fit and they know of such opportunities. Some of the folks that you interview with might have even come through the ranks as an intern themselves. Many companies also give cash rewards to their employees that find good candidates that come on board after their referral, so they are motivated financially to help you join their organization if they find you desirable. You might even find a mentor with whom you can build a longer-term relationship. People, especially alums from your own institution, love to give back and help others. Why not let the beneficiary of that desire be you?

Other resources are already likely available through your school. Engagement is key. Take advantage of your school's Career Services Office. They have skilled professionals that keep in touch with employers and the latest trends in the career field. They are often aware of a variety of opportunities. Your faculty is also usually engaged with professionals in their field. If you are seeking a marketing role, talk to your marketing faculty. Looking for accounting, talk to your accounting professor. Even your school's dean is likely to be well-connected within the community. Believe it or not, almost everybody you interact with wants you to succeed. Many schools have community advisory boards that bring back local professionals and alums wanting to enhance connections with people to their companies. On-campus clubs often bring community members onto campus. If you are an officer in the club or just attend meetings and open houses, you will have multiple opportunities to engage with current professionals and potential employers. Take advantage of these activities. Better yet, if you become an officer in a school organization, you may have opportunities to reach out directly to these community members and form a professional relationship when working to get them involved in your campus activities. When the time comes and they are looking for a student to fill a role in their organization, who do you think they might call?

Practice, practice, practice is more than just a saying, it enhances your capability and comfort level in networking and interviewing. I always tell my people, "The best time to attend a job fair is when you are not looking for a job or internship!" The reason why is that just having the experience, without the pressure of needing to find a position, will help you get more comfortable talking with professionals. You ideally do not want to participate in these activities when you are under pressure to find a role or desperate. Not only will that add stress to your interactions, but your level of confidence and comfort, if you have not participated in these types of activities previously, will likely be very low. The more experience and practice you get, the less nervous you will be and the better you will be able to perform. This sets you apart from others competing for the same role.

You also ultimately want to pursue multiple internships. Finding things you like and developing professional skills are powerful incentives to get an internship. As previously mentioned, finding things you don't like, be it environments, industries, corporate cultures, or types of work, will help you determine the things you do not want and helps you ultimately focus on the things you prefer to do. You also can get an internship after graduation. The author's oldest daughter had an internship at Rush Medical Center in Chicago that started the summer after her graduation. It so happens that she was planning on graduate school in Baltimore, but many do not intend to go to grad school and can still get an internship right after graduation that would often lead to a full-time position.

>>> (Optional) You can go to the online course workbook. and complete the exercise: Finding internship opportunities. This is part of an online course Module 6 Seeking, Finding, and Applying for Internships Exercise

Post-Internship Getting Hired

You have one foot in the door. How do you kick it down to get an offer, assuming there are job opportunities post-internship (which there usually are)? Bottom line, perform! Performance encompasses a lot of skills. Engage, volunteer, learn, network, ask questions, socialize (but don't overdo it), and actively take advantage of opportunities for growth and learning offered. Be positive and polite to all. Just like when you go for an interview, everybody, from the receptionist to the cleaning crew, can and does observe your activities.

Treating all with respect will be a positive reflection on you and earn you respect. Hiring is a two-way street. You are evaluating the company to see if it might be a good fit for you and your aspirations. They evaluate you to see if you might be a good long-term fit with their organization. The big advantage is you are already there. The employer has had a chance to gauge your work ethic and performance. You want them to want you. The best way to accomplish this is to take the initiative and go above and beyond, demonstrating your commitment and your worth.

One of my people had an amazing job experience. Working right underneath the controller of a smaller company, he was exposed to virtually all facets of accounting operations. He loved working with them. They loved his attitude and engagement. He learned a lot from the experience…and they offered him a position after graduation. When I asked him if he was going to take it, he said "No." The well-thought-out reason given was that the controller, who had been there about seven years, would be the next job that he would want to fill at this small company, and it was unlikely that the existing controller would be leaving when he would be ready. My next question naturally flowed to "So how's the search for your second internship". With the high rates of being offered a job after your internship, wouldn't you want to have two offers and decide rather than have one and feel obligated to take it?

Congratulations! You found the ideal internship opportunity. You realize the value of internships and the experience you will gain. You understand how these experiences will enhance your resume and LinkedIn profile while also giving you perspective when you return to the classroom. You might have even discovered some new interests while expanding your base of experiences and network. Let's make sure your job search toolkit is well-rounded with the other skills you want to have developed in getting hired!

Chapter Summary

- Having experience as an intern allows you to gain insight to help you determine if the job is a right fit for you.

- Having multiple internships gives you more opportunities

to try it out" to see that the job you are thinking about doing and the career you are thinking about having is the right fit for you.

- The more internships you have, the better chance of you getting hired.

AI ChatBot/ChatGPT Question:

The Question:
What is the best way to find paid internships?

The AI Response:
The best way to find paid internships is to research online job boards, search through your network of contacts, and apply directly to companies you are interested in. You can also search for postings on social media, university career centers, and internship placement programs. Additionally, attending job fairs and virtual career events can help you find paid internships.

Author's Comment on AI Response:
With an estimated 80% of jobs AND internships being found through networking, leveraging your network, including friends, parents of friends, faculty, club advisors, temple/church groups, and organizations that you might volunteer for, is a powerful way to seek and find opportunities. School-focused job boards like Handshake and Purple Briefcase, are also invaluable as you develop leads on where to seek opportunities. Pursue those opportunities with vigor! Invest the time and the return on that investment will be amazing.

7 DETERMINE THE WHERE TO SEEK OPPORTUNITIES

Researching and finding organizations/companies/industries that fit YOU.

"Don't be afraid to go out on a limb. That's where the fruit is."
H. Jackson Browne, Author of Life's Little Instruction Book

What this chapter covers:

- Researching organizations/companies/industries
- Networking/ADDITIONAL informational interviews
- Job shadowing
- Mentorship
- Corporate culture
- Matching you with the desired environment where you can excel.
- Are you willing/able to relocate or do you prefer to work remotely?
- Focus your search --- the scattergun approach, also known as "spray and pray" is not as effective.
- Are school resources available? - Career service offices, Handshake/Purple Briefcase/Other online platforms, career fairs, career tools, classes, seminars, workshops, faculty, alumni
- Other 3rd party tools - Glassdoor, Indeed, Monster.com, CareerBuilder, Industry organizations, LinkedIn, Robert Half, Zip Recruiter, Simply Hired, and Google for Jobs.
- Outreach to decision-makers - Letter of Interest

Now that you have a compass helping to guide you to your north star, and you have discovered what your true values are that are the foundation of your passion and purpose, we are ready to begin the search for the company matching your values, passion, and purpose. The search for where you find this open position begins with conversations and internet research.

Typing keywords into the Google search bar gets you a list of possible websites that will give you the information you seek. An AI query also provides a wonderful sounding board as you explore areas of interest.

For example, someone wants to research companies, organizations, and industries in Finance and Insurance

Here is what this internet search bar would look like:

You will notice that this search result includes a list of Financial Services organizations, along with questions and answers. Google Search results become a wealth of knowledge for any industry or career search.

Now, let's say that in this search you find [Company name] appealing as a place you might want to contribute your time, talent, passion, and purpose. So, there are at least three ways you can continue this research.

One way is to go on the website of [Company name] and read about them, their culture, their team, and the open career positions. You might also want to read about the various products and services and their special programs.

In other words, get to know the company as much as possible!

Another way to get to know all you can about the company is to go to its social media sites, starting with LinkedIn.

Type the company name: [company name] in the LinkedIn search bar (hit the enter key)

Then, click on the underline and see the LinkedIn [company name] website:

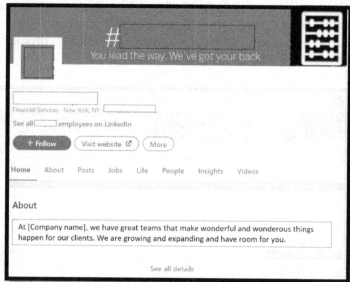

If you are serious about working on their team someday, it

is highly recommended that you Follow this company.

Now, see everything About this company. Read the posts. See the jobs, but before applying to them, read about the life you can look forward to working on the [Company name] team.

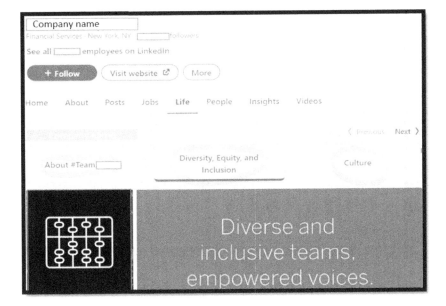

While you are reading about the team, the DEI, and the culture, take notes on a separate sheet of paper or in a Word document. You will refer back to this information as you engage in the application and interview process.

After reading up on their company, the team, and culture, be sure and view the videos and read about the insights. What you learn from this is worth "gold" to you for the application and interview!

Next, look to see the People.

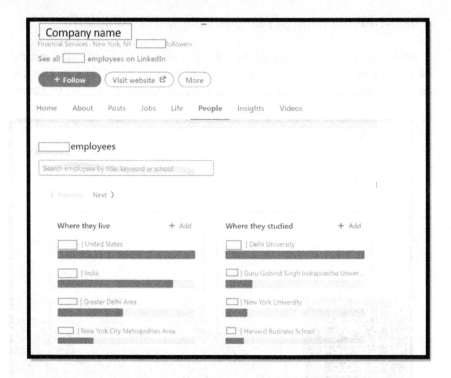

LinkedIn shows you that there is over [number] employees. You can identify where they live, where they studied, what they do, what they are skilled at, what they studied, and how you might be connected to any of them. (Use the Next and Previous arrows)

You can even click on the bar of any part of the graphic and it will take you to the list of people matching the statistics.

For example, here is a partial list of the people who studied at Harvard Business School:

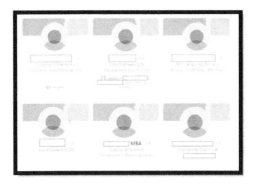

You can click on any of these people and read their LinkedIn profiles. This gives you some valuable insight into the education and training these people have and what you might need to obtain or have already obtained.

Now that you have researched the company, its culture, and the people, you are ready to move forward with what internship/job opportunities might be available.

Depending on what you learn about the open job positions, you might want to go to the list of personnel that best matches that position while applying (we will cover more on that in the next chapter).

School Connections/Resources

There may be someone working in the position you want to be working in that went to your school. Contacting them gives you an instant connection and instant common ground. When making this connection, it is recommended you use verbiage like this.

Hi, (person's full name), Enjoyed learning about your career path from your LinkedIn profile (or from wherever you found out about them) since graduation from (institution abbreviation). My name is (your full name). As a fellow (school mascot) I would be honored to connect with you. I am in my (college year) and am pursuing a (degree program. My goal after graduation is to be working in a (name the position or field you want to work in) and would appreciate the opportunity to connect and explore your path to success.

In appreciation,

(your first name)

****

Job Shadowing

Making a connection via LinkedIn is a great way to begin finding the person to ask questions. In a way, this is the kind of information gathering you would expect if you were spending the day shadowing the person.

However, by building a relationship with someone working for the company in the job position you are pursuing, you may be able to get together in person for an extended period of time, or possibly even a whole day, shadowing this person. This provides a great way to see if the job is something you would enjoy. Remember, the goal is to be in a job position where you ARE NOT WORKING IN but are CONTRIBUTING WITH COMPENSATION.

3rd Party Sites

Monster.com, CareerBuilder.com, and ZipRecruiter are the three major "generic" job sites. Unfortunately, they are saturated and even over-saturated with many fake job openings. These websites used to be the "go to" sites when seeking employment, and advertisers know this and started using these sites like billboard sites. Not only that but the job openings may already be filled and there is no way of telling. These sites invite you to "apply" for jobs. In doing so, you might also open yourself to continuous emailing and spam.

What we want you to do is get noticed. Statistically, your application to jobs is not as effective using these sites as you are making connections and having inside knowledge of the company you wish to work for. This is why it is important to know what job is best suited for you and you for it, and then to actively pursue current and future open (and sometimes unannounced) job positions.

There are thousands of applicants on these 3rd party sites. What this means is your pool of competition is deep and broad. It is usually more effective to go directly to the company website, see their position openings, and apply directly to the company.

Outreach to decision-makers

With a letter of intent for higher-level job positions, it is possible to gauge the level of interest regarding your job candidacy for a specific position. The higher the level, typically, the more steps in the process of applying for the position. This is more common with the C-Suite positions (CEO, CFO, COO, etc.) which are usually handled by a Search Committee. There are multiple levels of interviews, visits, and presentations that take place before a candidate is selected for and offered the position.

>>> (Optional) You can go to the online course workbook. and complete the exercise: Seeking 3 companies. This is part of an online course Module 6 Seeking, Finding, and Applying for Internships Exercise.

Chapter Summary

- Researching the company is a must-do.

- Seeking a company with the desired job position is the main goal for getting a career job.

- Making connections for getting on the inside of the company is a great way to start building relationships with people you might be working with in the future.

- Where you land a career job depends on what is best suited to you, your passion, and your purpose.

The Question:
What are the best resources to use to research a company when considering employment with them?

The AI Response:

1. Visit the company's website and read any available information.

2. Check Glassdoor to read company reviews and feedback from current and former employees.

3. Research the company's financials and history by looking at news articles, press releases, and SEC filings.

4. Reach out to current employees or alumni of the company and ask them questions.

5. Follow the company on social media to get a better understanding of their culture.

6. Look up any awards or recognition the company has received.

7. Read any blog posts or articles written by current or former employees.

Author's Comment on AI Response:

Not a bad starting point. Not sure how they missed using LinkedIn but will forgive them. By now, I know you can appreciate its immense value in exploring companies, finding out the backgrounds of people you might be interviewing with as well as facts about their C-suite management team, and as a source to find potential informational interview candidates. Two other secret (or not-so-secret) weapons should be mentioned. 1. Create a Google Alert (Google it ☐) on the company so that current information is automatically sent to your email. 2. To REALLY differentiate yourself, go to the SEC's (Securities and Exchange Commission) EDGAR website at https://www.sec.gov/edgar and do a company search. That site gives you access to ALL U.S. publicly traded companies and their annual report, known as a 10-K, which includes financial statements and lots of background information. Usually, the CEO or another senior executive includes an address about the company's current performance and anticipated future.

8 SEEKING, FINDING, APPLYING

Where do I go?

What this chapter covers:

- Seeking - Networking /job boards - (general, specific)
- Finding - Discovering the company with the job position
- Applying - keywords and the ATS
- Don't disqualify yourself --- pay attention to embedded instructions from HR
- Go to the company career website (not too fast with the blue button)
- Follow up with HR after you apply (who am I meeting with, do your LinkedIn diligence)

- Determine salary ranges for positions desired (geographic tools)
- Practice, practice, practice

The process of seeking a company and finding a matching job position is simple, yet most people make it complex. Believe it or not, the first thing to do is "google it."

SEEK and FIND

When you know the title of the job position you wish to have, all you need to do is type it in the search box at Google.

work at home data entry

The reason why we recommend Google Search and not any others is that Google has the most well-developed search engine. That could change, but presently, Google is the way to go. Wil be interesting to see how AI plays out in the search space with the integration of Google's Bard and Microsoft's GPT-4 into the mix.

Now that you have the job type in the search bar and click "enter," you will see the results. At the top of the results, you instantly see that you were not the only person on the planet wanting to search for a work-at-home data entry position. These search results show that you were one in 2 billion people worldwide looking to work at home entering data.

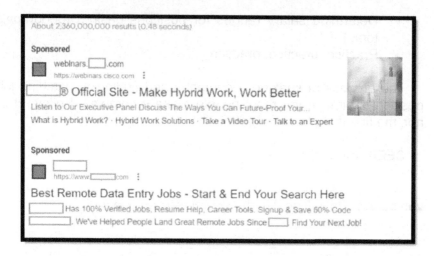

The next observation is the Sponsored ads. Be careful not to click on these. Having paid advertising listings, they are often not as they seem and can be misleading. The next thing to know is that you must never click on the hyperlink that says 100+ more jobs (this is a scam)

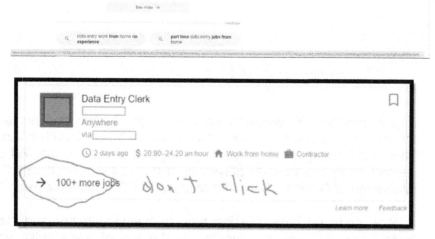

Look at the bottom of the screen while you hover your mouse — there are special characters, capital letters, random letters, and numbers strewn from left to right >>> this is a sign that if you click on this link, you are likely to go places you did not intend.

Please take heed of what we are teaching you. We are teaching you what you need to know so that you do not get scammed.

Speaking of being scammed, look at these icons. They usually appear at the bottom of the page. When you hover over them, see the strewn characters just like when hovering over the hyperlink: 100+ more jobs. These icons are of websites that were fabricated.

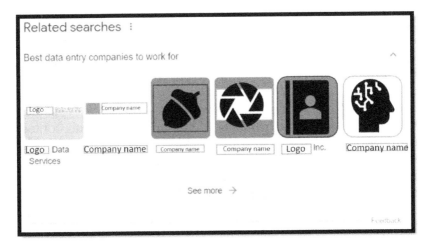

Note: There are many ways that this search is dangerous and a threat to be scammed. So, please pay close attention.

Moving forward and looking at the list of options in the search result, you see the link to Indeed. This is safe since Indeed carefully vets the postings to be sure you are applying for a real job from a real company. They are 99.9% legitimate in their postings.

Note the list of questions people also ask. You can take some time to see the answers if you like. If you want to get to seeking and finding the perfectly matched position for you to apply quickly, it is recommended you skip over these questions and answers for the time being.

Most people see that the job title they are looking for is listed on a site such as Indeed. There is a reason why Indeed is referred to as the #1 job site in the United States, and this is because for the past two decades, Indeed has had the largest amount of online, work-at-home jobs. Another reason is that it has a very effective resume builder that is open to employers. Many people we know got jobs via Indeed.

Going to Indeed, there is a process by which you can locate the company with the desired job position very easily and without being scammed.

The steps in the process are these, and will be discussed in detail:

Step 1: Google search (again, be careful with the hyperlinks)

Some of the hyperlinks are meant to be scams. Some of the hyperlinks are intended to lead you astray and take you places on the internet that you likely do not want to go.

To ensure you are safe, please watch the <u>bottom of your screen</u> when you hover over a hyperlink. If the URL is long and contains a bunch of characters including special characters, numbers, and letters, DO NOT CLICK IT. Be very careful of the bottom or top of the Google search results showing you icons and logos of companies you are familiar with. They are more than likely counterfeit websites and will not be good for you if you click on them.

To be sure, there are plenty of links you will come across that are not threatening. All you need to do is to watch the bottom of your screen when hovering over a hyperlink, and you can keep from being scammed or led astray on the internet.

NOW BACK TO THE STEPS:
Step 2: Go to Indeed (make sure the link is short and does not appear at the bottom of your screen as described in Step 1.)
Step 3: Make sure the location is remote if you want to work-at-home, and that the location is where you want to work onsite.

Step 4: Make sure the filter for the job being full-time, part-time, or temporary is properly set.

Step 5: See the search results.

Step 6: Carefully go over the search results, making sure to display the job description.

Step 7: <u>Read over the JOB REQUIREMENTS FIRST!</u> You can save a significant amount of time by going directly to the job requirements FIRST, before reading the job description from the top to the bottom. There may be more requirements. Be sure to read them too, making sure you meet these requirements.

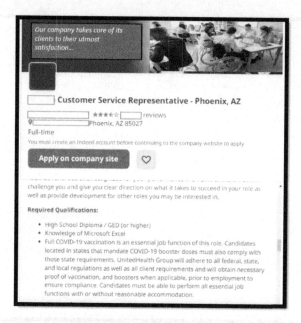

Our company takes care of its clients to their utmost satisfaction...

Customer Service Representative - Phoenix, AZ

★★★☆ reviews

Phoenix, AZ 85027

Full-time

You must create an Indeed account before continuing to the company website to apply

Apply on company site ♡

challenge you and give you clear direction on what it takes to succeed in your role as well as provide development for other roles you may be interested in.

Required Qualifications:

- High School Diploma / GED (or higher)
- Knowledge of Microsoft Excel
- Full COVID-19 vaccination is an essential job function of this role. Candidates located in states that mandate COVID-19 booster doses must also comply with those state requirements. UnitedHealth Group will adhere to all federal, state, and local regulations as well as all client requirements and will obtain necessary proof of vaccination, and boosters when applicable, prior to employment to ensure compliance. Candidates must be able to perform all essential job functions with or without reasonable accommodation.

Our company takes care of its clients to their utmost satisfaction...

Customer Service Representative - Phoenix, AZ

★★★☆ reviews

Phoenix, AZ 85027

Full-time

You must create an Indeed account before continuing to the company website to apply

Apply on company site ♡

and local regulations as well as all client requirements and will obtain necessary proof of vaccination, and boosters when applicable, prior to employment to ensure compliance. Candidates must be able to perform all essential job functions with or without reasonable accommodation.

Preferred Qualifications:

- Medical Terminology
- CPT and ICD - 9 coding
- Advanced knowledge of insurance products
- Advanced computer skills in Windows environment
- Training in a medical office or customer service-related field

Telecommuting Requirements:

- Reside within Phoenix, AZ

Our company takes care of its clients to their utmost satisfaction...

Customer Service Representative - Phoenix, AZ

★★★☆ eviews

Phoenix, AZ 85027

Full-time

You must create an Indeed account before continuing to the company website to apply

Apply on company site ♡

living areas and provides information privacy
- Ability to keep all company sensitive documents secure (if applicable)
- Must live in a location that can receive a UnitedHealth Group approved high-speed internet connection or leverage an existing high-speed internet service

Soft Skills:

- Ability to prioritize call types
- Strong and solid oral and written communication skills
- Ability to demonstrate customer service and proper telephone etiquette
- Solid listening, critical thinking, decision making, telephone, customer service and problem solving skills

requires all new hires and employees to report their COVID-19 vaccination status.

Step 8: Assuming you meet most of the job (Required, Preferred, Telecommuting, etc.) requirements, read the job description from the top to the bottom very closely and carefully.

Step 9: Assuming you agree with working in this job position, the next step is to "google the company." DO NOT HIT THE Blue APPLY BUTTON (unless directed)

***Make sure there are no embedded directions at the bottom or anywhere in the job description telling you to email or call someone. If you do not do as directed, YOU HAVE JUST DISQUALIFIED YOURSELF. ***

Do you see the statement to connect for a look behind-the-scenes of this company? What this means is you are expected to go to these social media sites and learn about the company's culture AND CONNECT WITH THEM. What do you suppose this means? If you are serious about being a candidate for this job position, and you are not connected to them as per directed? This is a method of candidacy elimination. Not only connect with them but take notes as you learn about them on social media. These notes come in handy as you write the cover letter (if requested) or answer essay questions that are on the online application form and prepare for the job interview. Human Resource hiring professionals want to spend time and effort only on job applicants that take the time to follow directions and learn about their company and culture. If you are really serious about wanting to join their team, you will want to take the time to connect with them on their social media sites. If you really want to impress them and gain more points, search for this company on Google and see if you can see them in the news of their industry. The more news articles you read, the more relevant a job candidate you become to them!

Make sure that you do not miss out on a job opportunity by accidentally disqualifying yourself as a job candidate. Read the entire job description or you could miss what is highlighted.

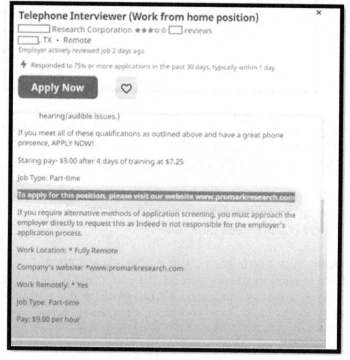

If you apply for this position by clicking the blue Apply Now, you are not following their directions and have automatically disqualified yourself.

If you are seeking a work-at-home position, be sure that you reside in the state for which they are hiring.

We offer Remote Inside Sales positions in 31 states- AL, AZ, CO, FL, GA, IA, ID, IN, KS, MD, MI, MN, MO, NC, ND, NE, NH, NJ, NM, NV, PA, OK, OR, RI, SC, TX, UT, VA, VT, WA, WI. Please visit our website to apply to an opening in one of these other states:
https://jobs.libertymutualgroup.com/careers/css/inside-sales/

Now moving forward to the next step.

DON'T DISQUALIFY YOURSELF

Qualifications:
Qualified candidates will have 2 years of recent customer service experience and a consistent job history
Must be able to successfully work in a fast-paced environment while maintaining a professional, courteous, and helpful attitude
Excellent oral communication skills and telephone etiquette
Ability to identify high level customer issues to be escalated to a Team Lead
Demonstrated hand-eye coordination for P.C. work, and the ability to speak and listen via the telephone
Computer skills and demonstrated sound-decision making skills a must!
You enjoy being of service to others before yourself
Retail or guest service experience in the service industry
Show us your fabulous smile while multi-tasking in a fast paced environment
Flexible schedule including evenings, weekends, and holidays
Comfortable keyboarding in a windows based environment

Connect with us for a behind-the-scenes look at the Mario Tricoci culture on Facebook, Twitter, and Instagram

https://www.instagram.com/mariotricoci/

https://www.facebook.com/MarioTricociHairSalonsDaySpas/
Tricoci Salon & Spa

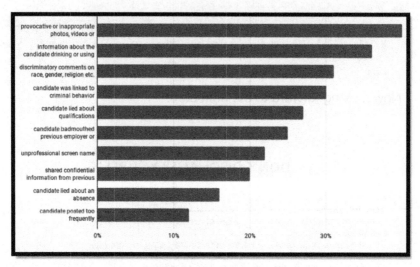

https://toggl.com/blog/social-media-screening

If you apply for this position by clicking the blue Apply Now, you are not following their directions and have automatically disqualified yourself.

If you are seeking a work-at-home position, be sure that you reside in the state for which they are hiring.

Step 10: <u>Google the company and make sure it is real and not fake.</u> Look for errors in spelling and grammar and look to make sure the phone numbers on the website are real. If the website does not have a Privacy Statement or Terms of Use, stay away. A sure sign this is real is when there is evidence of endorsements by others in the same industry.

Step 11: Read ABOUT the Company and all there is to know about the company from the entire website. After all, you want to know what to expect as a member of the team in the company.

Step 12: Use AI tools like ChatGPT-3.5/GPT-4 to analyze the company, its website, and its mission/vision/values/culture.

To achieve our mission...

We seek to enhance the performance of the health system and improve the overall health and well-being of the people we are privileged to serve and their communities.

We work with health care professionals and other key partners to expand access to high-quality health care so people get the care they need at an affordable price.

We support the physician/patient relationship and empower people with the information, guidance and tools they need to make personal health choices and decisions.

Our mission in action

Learn how our team members across [   ] and [   ] are working to help build a modern, high-performing health system that improves access, affordability, outcomes and experiences for the people who depend on it.

Keep reading →

Integrity. We are dedicated to the highest levels of personal and institutional integrity. We make honest commitments and work to consistently honor those commitments. We do not compromise ethics. We strive to deliver on our promises and we have the courage to acknowledge mistakes and do whatever is needed to address them.

Compassion. We try to walk in the shoes of the people we serve and the people we work with across the health care community. Our job is to listen with empathy and then respond appropriately and quickly with service and advocacy for each individual, each group or community and for society as a whole. We celebrate our role in serving people and society in an area so vitally human as their health.

Relationships. We build trust through cultivating relationships and working in productive collaboration with governments, employers, physicians, nurses and other health care professionals, hospitals and the individual consumers of health care. Trust is earned and preserved through truthfulness, integrity, active engagement and collaboration with our colleagues and clients. We encourage the variety of thoughts and perspectives that reflect the diversity of our markets, customers and workforce.

Innovation. We pursue a course of continuous, positive and practical innovation, using our deep experience in health care to be thoughtful advocates of change and using the insights we gain to invent a better future that will make the health care environment work and serve everyone more fairly, productively and consistently.

Performance. We are committed to deliver and demonstrate excellence in everything we do. We will be accountable and responsible for consistently delivering high-quality and superior results that make a difference in the lives of the people we touch. We continue to challenge ourselves to strive for even better outcomes in all key performance areas.

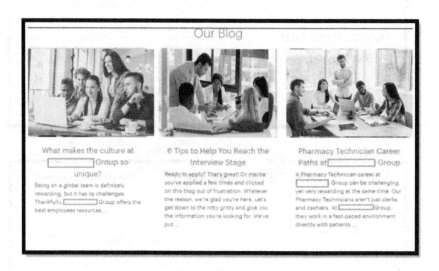

Use this matrix to notate important facts about the company.

Company name	Mission	Purpose	Values	Latest news

>>> (Optional) You can go to the online course workbook. and

complete the exercise: Seeking 3 companies with finding 3 viable job positions you may want to apply to, This is part of an online course Module 8 Matching with 3 Companies assignment.

Step 12: Check the CAREERS page. You might be surprised to learn that the job posted on Indeed has already been filled. But, if it is still open, and you want to work on it, then proceed with the next steps in the application process.

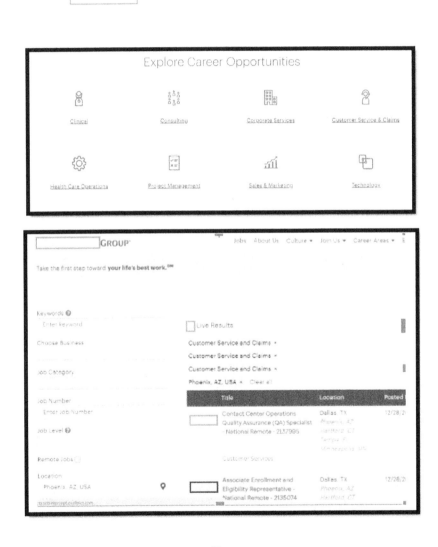

APPLY

The application process varies according to the company and its ways of handling the hiring process. Usually, there are some commonalities to this process. One of them is making sure you have a resume that showcases your accomplishments WITH metrics. It paints a picture in the mind of the hiring authority as to how you work. Lastly, this also gives them a bird's eye view of your consistency in working in the field (which shows the level of your expertise and experience).

Having a resume is one element of the POWER OF 3.

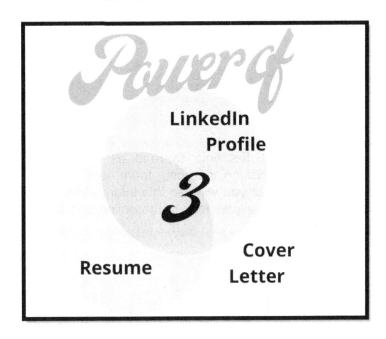

The "Power of 3" happens when your LinkedIn profile, resume, and cover letter (or online application questions or essays are aligned perfectly). When all three of these elements are good to go you are more than likely to get contacted for an interview.

You, as a job candidate, must show the hiring authority that you are the right choice and best candidate for the position. Most people start with their resume, but we tell people to make sure to have their LinkedIn profile to the All-Star level completing all the sections. Having recommendations and endorsements in your LinkedIn profile adds power as well. When the LinkedIn profile is ready to be seen, then it is time to write the resume. The resume is covered in detail in the next chapter.

Sometimes, the company will give you their hiring process to adjust your expectations. Consider this a gift to you.

Our Hiring Process

We want you to know what our hiring process looks like.

Before you begin your career search with [_____] Group, find out what to expect along the way.

Learn more about our hiring process

- You must take the time to read all there is about the company, its mission, purpose, team, and the latest news. >>Take notes as you will use this information in your cover letter, answers to questions in the online application, and in your interview(s).

Chapter Summary

- It takes time to seek and find the company with the job position you are most qualified and interested in.

- A Google Search is the best place to start (making sure not to be scammed or led astray).

- When you find the job description on Indeed, you must know beyond a doubt that the job and the company are real.

You must take the time to read all there is about the company, its mission, purpose, team, and the latest news. >>Take notes as you will use this information in your cover letter, answers to questions in the online application, and in your interview(s).

The Question:
What are the top 50 websites for job searching and their URLs?

The AI Response:

1. Indeed (www.indeed.com)
2. Glassdoor (www.glassdoor.com)
3. LinkedIn (www.linkedin.com)
4. Monster (www.monster.com)
5. CareerBuilder (www.careerbuilder.com)
6. TheLadders (www.theladders.com)
7. ZipRecruiter (www.ziprecruiter.com)
8. SimplyHired (www.simplyhired.com)

9. Craigslist (www.craigslist.org)
10. Dice (www.dice.com)
11. USAJobs (www.usajobs.gov)
12. FlexJobs (www.flexjobs.com)
13. SnagAJob (www.snagajob.com)
14. Jobsearch.com (www.jobsearch.com)
15. Job.com (www.job.com)
16. Beyond.com (www.beyond.com)
17. JobRapido (www.jobrapido.com)
18. JobFox (www.jobfox.com)
19. The Muse (www.themuse.com)
20. CareerJet (www.careerjet.com)
21. Jobster (www.jobster.com)
22. CollegeRecruiter (www.collegerecruiter.com)
23. Job Bank USA (www.jobbankusa.com)
24. GovernmentJobs (www.governmentjobs.com)
25. Job.net (www.job.net)
26. JobCircle (www.jobcircle.com)
27. Jobs.com (www.jobs.com)
28. Resume-Library (www.resume-library.com)
29. JobisJob (www.jobisjob.com)
30. JobOpenings (www.jobopenings.net)
31. Job.com.au (www.job.com.au)
32. JobNab (www.jobnab.com)
33. VetJobs (www.vetjobs.com)
34. EmploymentGuide (www.employmentguide.com)
35. JobGob (www.jobgob.com)
36. Trovit (www.trovit.com)
37. JobSearchUSA (www.jobsearchusa.org)
38. Snag (www.snag.com)
39. Geebo (www.geebo.com)
40. CareerBliss (www.careerbliss.com)
41. Jobing (www.jobing.com)
42. Jobs.ie (www.jobs.ie)
43. Jobswire (www.jobswire.com)
44. JobFetch (www.jobfetch.com)
45. MyJob (www.myjob.com)
46. JobStreet (www.jobstreet.com)
47. JobSearchMonitor (www.jobsearchmonitor.com)
48. JobisJob (www.jobisjob.co.uk)
49. JobSearchTexas (www.jobsearchtexas.com)
50. Careers.org (www.careers.org)

Author's Comment on AI Response:

Reminder: Networking is STILL the best way to find opportunities. Don't let job boards be your only source of job leads. Warning: Be careful not to just "spray and pray" when applying. You can easily apply for over 100 jobs in less than an hour with the one-click option found in many of the mentioned sites, but your chance of landing an interview, without further follow-up, is virtually 0%. A couple of other sources to consider, if you are willing to take on temporary work for fun, profit, or experience, check out Fiverr, Upwork, and Freelancer.

9 RESUME TEMPLATE

Customization is king and queen.

"You can get everything in life you want if you will just help enough other people get what they want."
Zig Ziglar, Author and Motivational Speaker

What this chapter covers:

- Do I need to customize to different jobs?
- Formatting and Length.

- Use LinkedIn to Build A Resume.
- What to include and not include.
- Metrics must be included.
- Celebrate your victories.
- Ethical considerations.

Many years ago, it was the prevailing method to write a resume with five sections and let that be "one and done." The resume was printed on parchment paper with 100 copies made and then was given to hiring managers who posted "help wanted" signs in the window. Ah, the good ole days when getting a job was as "easy" as making it known you were available for the job equipped with the level of education, experience, expertise, and enthusiasm required to impress the hiring official. Okay, it was never that easy. Today, it is even less simple. Today, employers want their hiring officials to be sure that the people they select are meeting all the requirements to join their team and can go the distance with the interviewing and onboarding processes. Social media sites have become the landscape for job posters and job seekers to find each other. Now, to get a decent-paying position, you must stand out from the crowd, brand yourself as an attractive candidate, and have social and experiential proof that you are the right person for the role. Wow, how you might wish for the times of the good ole days.

Nevertheless, at present, a job seeker deemed attractive to employers has taken the time and energy to create for themselves a means by which they are discovered and sought after by hiring officials. How this is done is what this chapter is all about.

We first begin by answering the question most people ask: "Do I really need more than one resume?" The answer is YES. In fact, you need a resume that is customized to each specific job posting to which you are responding. Not only that, but your LinkedIn profile must align perfectly with what your resume says so that the hiring official has a clear picture in their mind as to the capability, capacity, and character of you. We have heard from Human Resource hiring managers that they often go to the LinkedIn profile to learn what they need to know about a candidate 95% after the resume passes the screening at an automated reader (The ATS - Applicant Tracking System). They said that after glancing at the LinkedIn profile (for about 30 seconds, but usually closer to 10 seconds), they determined the person is matching with who they are seeking and then reached out to them to schedule an interview. This only happens when the resume and LinkedIn profile are aligned and satisfy the needs of the hiring official and their organization.

Formatting and Length

Experts and professionals have strongly recommended resumes be between one and two pages, and no more than two pages; use only one page if possible. The format needs to be simplistic and there are about the same number of human resources hiring managers that prefer the resume not to be from a template, versus those who are neutral on the resume being from a resume template. It is highly recommended the formatting of the resume:

- Be in the same font throughout the resume.
- Use headers that are in a slightly larger font and bolded.
- Have no spelling and grammar errors.
- No gaps in employment (fill gap periods with volunteering)
- Include proof of impact (showing metrics of accomplishments)
- Exclude specific street addresses (city and state are appropriate)
- Not include references or the statement: "Reference available upon request."

One thing they all say is that they look at the resume wanting proof this person has what it takes to contribute to the team with excellence. They get this proof with the metrics of accomplishment and the consistency of employment and/or volunteerism.

Use LinkedIn to Build a Resume

LinkedIn has a feature allowing you to build your resume using the LinkedIn resume builder. It is a great way to ensure your resume and LinkedIn Profile match perfectly. It is also an easy and user-friendly method that is stored in your profile and visible to potential employers. A quick way to grammar/spell checks your LinkedIn profile is to generate your profile as a pdf, and then run this content through a tool like https://grammarly.com/,

What to Include and What Not to Include on Your Resume
Every resume is customized to the job description. Look for keywords in the job description. These are exactly the words to use in your resume. You want to be sure that you are listing jobs you did

in the past and present that align with the job you seek to fill. For example, if you wish to fill a retail customer service position, you will want all the retail store positions listed on the resume, not the jobs you did that were not related to retail. Doing this may cause a gap in the chronology of your work experience, but this can be explained in a cover letter or a comment section on the online job application.

Here are some Do's and Don'ts for writing an effective resume.

Do
List your past and present job positions beginning with the recent job position.
Follow the chronology of employment time in descending order.
Include a list of skill sets (if there is room) - if not, the LinkedIn Profile will have them for the hiring professional to see.
Include the keywords used in the job description as much as possible (authentically),

Don't
Have spelling and grammar errors.
List jobs without metrics
List references
Have more than five bullet points per past or present job position
Unexplained gaps in employment

Metrics of Accomplishment

What we mean when we say, "metrics of accomplishment" is simply answering the question, "What impact did you make while performing your work tasks?" Depending on the level of your responsibility, this impact will be small or large. The metrics of your accomplishment reflect this impact. Here are some examples:

An Insurance Salesperson applying for a sales manager position might have these metrics:

- Increased corporate sales accounts from 10 per month to 20 per month.
- Increased the sales revenue by 45% each year of tenure.
- Increased the number of clients enrolling in plans by 23%
- Decreased the number of clients failing to pay premiums by

35%

Someone applying for a manager position might have these metrics:
- Led a sales team to increase sales revenue by 45%
- Increased the number of team members' professional certifications.
- Decreased the number of people leaving our company.

This gives the hiring official a glimpse of what you have contributed in the past and will likely contribute in the future for their company/organization.

Celebrate Your Victories

What this means is you have contributed toward the success of others, and you are proud of that. If you are just out of high school and entering college for the first time, you may wonder if this statement applies to you. IT DOES. As you play sports or enter competitions, you are a team player and a contributor. As such, when your team won a game, match, debate, or competition or stood tall on stage for a screenplay or musical, you were a part of that. BE PROUD.

Not only does pride enter into this, but you can leverage those moments as you are writing your resume.

Ethical Considerations

DO NOT FAKE INFORMATION ON A RESUME. This is committing fraud. The last thing you want to do is commit fraud at any time in your lifetime. This is misrepresenting yourself and WHEN caught, termination is likely. This is also potentially a crime punishable with fines and/or prison.

>>> (Optional) You can go to the online course workbook. and complete the exercise: Metrics of your accomplishments. This is part of an online Module 9 Writing a Resume Exercises Workbook.

Chapter Summary

- A resume is one element in the Power of 3.
- An effective resume is only one to two pages and is formatted in the same font.
- An effective and powerful resume has metrics of accomplishments in bullet points and has keywords consistent with the job description.
- A resume with gaps in employment includes periods of volunteerism.

The Question:
What are the top 25 mistakes job candidates make when creating their resumes?

The AI Response:
1. Incorrect or outdated contact information
2. Poorly organized resume
3. Unprofessional font choice
4. Not optimizing for Applicant Tracking Systems (ATS)
5. Too much information
6. Not emphasizing accomplishments
7. Failing to tailor your resume to the job description
8. Not using action verbs
9. Not quantifying achievements
10. Too much jargon
11. Not including relevant keywords
12. Not explaining employment gaps
13. Not including a cover letter
14. Not providing references
15. Not proofreading
16. Not including or emphasizing volunteer experience
17. Not formatting for readability
18. Not customizing your resume for each job
19. Not including relevant skills
20. Not highlighting transferrable skills
21. Not including certifications or awards
22. Not emphasizing soft skills
23. Not including a profile/summary section
24. Not formatting for a one-page resume
25. Not including online profiles (e.g., LinkedIn)

Author's Comment on AI Response:
Though somewhat generic in response to typical ChatGPT style, some of the tips are reasonable to consider like including keywords

for the ATS from the job description and tailoring your resume individually for each opportunity - yes time consuming, but worth it! Others you may want to disregard such as formatting for one page or needing to include references. Another tip regarding contact information is that you typically do not want to include your full address. Usually, city, state, and zip in the U.S. are all you want to share for security and a variety of other reasons. Also, remember that all rules have exceptions. You also want to make sure you match your resume to your LinkedIn profile, especially dates (if included). Your LinkedIn profile can have more information, but it does need to be consistent with the resume. Your interviewer will also likely have your resume in front of them, and always bring extra copies in case you bump into folks that do not have it. Also, make sure your cover letter flows nicely with your resume.

SEE EXAMPLES OF RESUMES: https://www.indeed.com/career-advice/resume-samples

10 THE COVER LETTER

Do I need one?

What this chapter covers:

- Why do I need one?

- It's not about you ... but how you fit in with the company.

- Do your homework (how you know you fit)

- Time to shine (concisely)

- One page wonder (instrument to impress)

At present, some hiring professionals mandate cover letters and others do not. It depends on who you ask.

Why you might need a cover letter.

According to CNBC, cover letters are passe.[1] Only 58% of hiring professionals prefer job applicants to include a cover letter with their resume. But it is also interesting that in this same article, it was recommended you write one regardless of it being required. They said it is an extension of the resume.

Yet another article says that cover letters are needed. So unless you know which 58% of the hiring professionals prefer a cover letter, it is better to be prepared with a cover letter for most of your applications.

---

[1] https://www.cnbc.com/2022/10/13/most-workers-say-cover-letters-are-unnecessary-heres-when-to-write-one.html#:~:text=Only%2010%25%20of%20professionals%20say, way%20that%20resumes%20don't

Writing an effective cover letter takes research, reflection, and reassurance. Researching the job description, the company, and the culture of the company must come first. Taking notes on the key aspects of the culture, the company, and its mission, purpose, goals, and core values are crucial for writing the most effective cover letter and for preparing to meet with someone from human resources. AT tools can be used to summarize the above.

The resume gives a snapshot of what you have done and forms an impression of the skills you must do the job when you join the team. The cover letter gives more of a picture of how you fit with the company, its culture, and the career position.

Why there are so many more human resource professionals not preferring to use the cover letter as a means of shortening the candidacy pool, relates to the fact that most people do not know how to write a cover letter that gets, keeps, and attracts the attention of the hiring official.

It's not about you … it's about the company and how you fit with the company.

The cover letter gives you the privilege to demonstrate how well you match with the company (first) and the posted job position (second). The hiring professional is looking for the best candidate to fill the position. They want someone who fits best with their team. Consideration of this starts with determining the value of the candidate based on their compatibility with their company, and second, their capacity for contributing toward the success of the team they will be working with.

Do your Homework

The only way to demonstrate how well you fit in with the company and its culture is to know exactly what the culture is. This begins with understanding the mission, vision, goals, purpose, and values of the company. The candidate needs to know as much as possible about the people, product, service, and to whom the product and/or service is marketed. Understanding the customer perspective is needed too so that you can fully articulate how you best fit with the company and what the company does for its clients and/or customers.

The more information you can learn from the company's website and other resources, the more likely you will have the information to impress the hiring professional and the hiring manager. This information demonstrates the effort you made to seek the position and the depth to which you went to discover how you fit with the company.

Making a match between you and the company is what the cover letter facilitates. You need to write a cover letter that attracts the company to you and lays the foundation for a great and lasting relationship.

Most people start the cover letter with:

"I am applying for the customer service position having been a customer service representative for the past 10 years." — starting a cover letter like this does not distinguish you from your competition and starts out similar to most of the other candidates.

This is an example of a cover letter that has historically been super successful in getting asked for an interview!

XYZ company has an impressive track record for customer satisfaction with three core principles: integrity, honor, and precision. I too have a great customer satisfaction track record, award winning centered around the same three core principles. I love to help people and I always operate with integrity, honor, and precision making sure that everyone I meet and assist with meeting their needs smile and are super satisfied with the outcome. There are three occasions I wish to share that show this to be true.

Customer service satisfaction is paramount to me feeling fulfilled> When a customer complains about a product they received, I listen carefully, fullt empathize and then get to work to resolve the complaint. I know I did a great job when they say "thanks" with heartfelt gratitude. When a customer begins a conversation angry and leaves like we're friends, I know I did a great job. I have a customer following and this is another sign I am doing my best to help my customers and they appreciate me for it.

The customer service position with XYZ company fits perfectly for my character and your company's track record and core principles fits perfectly with where I would thrive. I look forward to the day we can meet.

In appreciation,

(you)

Time for You to Shine

If you wanted to have the work-at-home job as a Customer Service Representative working for UnitedHealth Group, here is how you would write the first two sentences.

Helping people live happier and healthier lives is what you as a company do and this is exactly what I have been doing in my capacity as a healthcare telehealth operator. For the past 10 years, every day, and in every way, I do my best to assist patients to have what they need, as they need it, operating with integrity and relating to them with compassion, and innovation, and providing excellent performance resulting in positive outcomes. As your Customer Service Representative, I will contribute to your continued success as the number one healthcare organization in the region.

Now, put yourself in the place of the human service hiring professional by reading the first two sentences of your cover letter. This cover letter gets read all-the-way through (no doubt).

It is a human principle in action. The more interest you show in someone or in a company, the more interested they become in the one showing interest in them!

Having a LinkedIn profile showing the education and experience that demonstrates competency, a resume that demonstrates capacity, and a cover letter that demonstrates cultural compatibility, helps the hiring professional to put you on the list to be interviewed.

Here is a snapshot of a text message that came to one of our clients 15 minutes after all three elements of the "Power of 3" were ready to go.

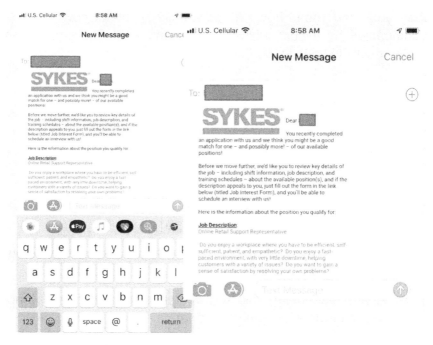

It took 30 minutes to build the LinkedIn profile, customize the resume, and write the 1.5-page cover letter. So, within 45 minutes, from start to finish, this client achieved a job interview that resulted in a job offer.

LinkedIn
Profile

3

Resume

Cover
Letter

Now you can see how a powerfully written cover letter, accompanied by a customized resume and well-aligned LinkedIn profile, results in a job interview.

>>> (Optional) You can go to the online course workbook. and complete the exercise: Powerful first sentence. This is part of an online course Module 10 Powerful First Sentence Assignment and Exercise.

Chapter Summary

- A cover letter is not needed as much now as in the past, but it is still a powerful tool

- A well-researched and well-written cover letter will attract and impress a hiring professional.

- The discovery of detailed company information facilitates the understanding of your fit within the company culture.

- Hiring professionals are attracted to job candidates that demonstrate their compatibility and capacity.

The Question:

What makes for a good cover letter and please demonstrate a sample.

The AI Response:

A good cover letter should be concise, professional, and tailored to the job you are applying for. It should include relevant information about your work experience, skills, and qualifications that make you a good fit for the role. Additionally, a cover letter should be well-written and free of errors. Finally, be sure to end your letter with a call to action and your contact information.

Sample Cover Letter:

Dear [Hiring Manager],

I am writing to express my interest in the [Position] role at [Company Name]. With my diverse background in [field], I believe I am well-suited to make an immediate and valuable contribution to your organization.

My current role as a [position title] at [current company] has provided me with extensive experience in [relevant skills]. I am comfortable working with multiple teams and stakeholders, and I am confident in my ability to quickly understand the needs of a new organization.

I am confident that I have the drive and ambition to be a great asset to your team. I am confident that I can bring the necessary skills and knowledge to ensure success in the role and to make a positive contribution to [Company Name].

Thank you for your time and consideration. I look forward to hearing from you about this opportunity.

Sincerely, [Your Name]

Author's Comment on AI Response:

Be careful when using a tool like ChatGPT to generate your "custom" cover letter. You do want it to be more personal, and tailored, and remember that the letter is about your FIT with the company to which you are applying. It is more about the solutions you bring to meet their needs, than about the skills you have in general. The cover letter's goal is to get you in the door. The interview is where you want to demonstrate those skills mentioned in your cover letter, resume, and LinkedIn profile.

11 SEIZE THE INTERVIEW AND OPTIMIZE IT

Putting your best confident foot forward.

"When you talk, you are only repeating what you already know. But if you listen, you may learn something new."

Dalai Lama

What this chapter covers:

- Prepare, prepare, prepare (Checklist).

- Types of interview (stress, behavioral, factual, etc.)

- Answering and asking questions.

- You are interviewing them too! (2-way interview).

- "2 ears, 1 mouth."

- Dress for Success.

- STAR Method.

- Stay CURIOUS.

- What's legal to ask?

After being contacted by the hiring professional, you simultaneously feel excited and filled with trepidation. Possibly you are a bit nervous to meet up with someone from the company you wish to work for and may have never met. But we do know that the more you know, the more likely you are to ace the interview and come away from it feeling upbeat and exhilarated.

Whatever the type of interview, the goals are multi-faceted. The company is looking to see that you not only have the skills to do the job but are also a good fit with the corporate culture and environment. As the interviewee, you have the same goals. In addition, both you and the company are in sales mode. They are not only checking you out, but they are trying to sell you on why you would want to work for their organization. You are doing the same emphasizing why you are the right person for the opportunity ready to make a difference at their organization.

An interview is usually more of a dialog. Interviewers tend to "feel" best about candidates that are engaging and can establish a two-way dialog. Having done your research and being able to ask intelligent questions, an interviewer will have the opportunity to share more about themselves and their company. This also demonstrates your interest and engagement in the potential position.

You also should realize that EVERYBODY you meet, from the receptionist to the janitor, is a potential interviewer. Of course, you want to impress the person or persons you are there to interview with, but rest assured, the impression you make on everyone counts so be on your best behavior.

You may have heard the expression "We have two ears and one mouth; we should be listening twice as much as talking". You of course will be answering lots of questions, but hopefully, you will be interacting and asking lots of questions too. When you can get the interviewer talking, it has been shown that they feel more positive about the interview and the candidate. Yes, people love talking about themselves, but it is also a great way to gain additional insights and understanding of the organization's environment. It can help you decide if and when you have multiple job offers which is the right role to accept.

Dress for Success

You probably don't want to wear a Harley Davidson tee shirt when you show up for your interview unless you are possibly applying at a dealership to be a tech. And even if that were the case you should probably still think twice. You definitely do not want to underdress for your interview, but is it possible to overdress? The short answer is yes!

Do you want to wear a tuxedo to the interview? You would surely stand out and make a statement, and if that is your intent and how you think you can best be remembered, go for it. How about showing up in a 3-piece suit or formal dress if you happen to be interviewing on a casual Friday? You would likely stand out and possibly feel uncomfortable. The bottom line is to do your homework. Find out about regular dress codes and special days. It is usually recommended to dress one step up so that if polo shirts are the standard, possibly a polo shirt with a blazer might be appropriate. Or if blazers and ties are fairly standard, a suit and tie or nicer dress could be appropriate. Power Tip: You also want to be aware of corporate colors, often seen in the logo, and try to integrate those colors into your outfit for the day.

Prepare, prepare, and prepare

When preparing for your job interview, this is where your note taking from researching and reading all the information you have from the company's website and other resources comes in handy. Some of our clients made columns of information and copied them into a Word document or Excel spreadsheet that they took with them to the interview.

If you were interviewing for the Customer Service job with United Health Group, here is what the interview prep sheet would look like:

Mission	Vision	Core Values	Who do they serve	Recent news

You want to pay attention to the company's involvement in environmental social governance (ESG) activities as a measure of their ethical and corporate social responsibility. Is this company giving back or taking away? Does it have a program that takes care of the environment including the planet and the people that live on it? Do they live their mission and foster that culture within their organization?

Most companies have foundations by which they donate to non-profit organizations that are serving the needs of people who are experiencing challenging situations. Some companies have an employee volunteer program that pays their employees to give their time and talent in support of a non-profit organization. If this is something of importance to the company and you, it adds to being a good fit.

Modalities of Job Interviews

Whether it is a phone interview, video, or face-to-face, you want to be prepared to impress. Maximizing the potential for your success means planning and setting up the appropriate environment. You have already done your research on the company and who you will be talking to.

Phone Interview

If you are having a telephone interview, you want to be in a quiet and comfortable place, well-rested, with a notepad in hand, so that you can focus on the person you are talking with. Some people prefer to stand during a phone interview as it gives them a bearing that comes through the phone as more confident. And yes, even in a phone interview, you want to SMILE!

Video Interview

When it comes to video interviews, you also want to be well-prepared and well-rested. The environment should be well thought out as to its visual and audio impact. This means proper lighting to put you in the best light - be careful of those windows where the sun might be coming in, as this can cause glare or fool your camera and make you look dark. You want to make sure you have quality audio! You say wait a minute, isn't this a video interview? It is but the video interview involves multiple senses, and not having good audio and video quality can be very distracting...and SMILE!

Face-to-Face Interview

In the face-to-face, your initial impression will be perceived by your appearance. Did you shower (note - no heavy perfume/cologne as some people have allergies and workplaces are becoming much more sensitive and aware of these considerations). Is hair and overall appearance neat and clean? Are your clothes ironed or pressed and not distracting? Are your shoes clean and shiny? Of course, you want to have a firm handshake and to SMILE when introduced. Similar to a resume, it is said that the first five seconds of interaction set the tone and impression when meeting someone for the first time. Make the best impression you can, it makes a difference.

Types of Job Interviews

There are many different types of job interviews. There may be only one person you meet, or several people at the same time in a panel interview. Regardless of the type of interview, the interrogatory is the same. The goal is also the same: Are you the right and best candidate for the job and would you be a good fit with the organization? Both of you are in sales mode to answer that question. You are also likely to be competing with other candidates, so you do want to stand out...in a positive way. The potential employer wants to get to know you, and you want to get to know them. Remember to always stay positive and SMILE!

Putting your best foot forward in an interview includes being prepared and understanding the motivations behind the multiple types of interviews. Let's look at some of the basic formats you could run into. Whatever the type, knowing the goals will help put you in the best light.

Informational Interview

This is less a job interview and more of a discovery opportunity about an organization, career path, as well as the person you are talking to. Worth repeating, these are not specifically job interviews but as previously discussed, are oriented to building rapport and gathering background information on the person you are talking to. You do not want to directly ask for a job. If the interviewer enjoys the experience and has good feelings about you, they will naturally mention opportunities they may know of or refer you to others that might be familiar with available opportunities.

Individual Interviews

Individual interviews allow for direct conversations and give both interviewer and interviewee the ability to dive deeper into areas that both want to discover more about. The interviewer, as mentioned above, is looking for a fit with the role and the organization. You, the interviewee, are seeking the same. You want to make sure you are ready by knowing as much as you can about the company and the interviewer. Not only will you hopefully have checked out the background of the interviewer on LinkedIn, along with the background of all other people you will be interviewing with. You want to have questions already written down based on your research. This helps greatly if you draw a blank when asked "Do you have any more questions." The worst answer to that question, besides "no" is "The information you shared is so complete, you were able to answer all of my questions during the interview". Such an accomplishment is not possible. Not having questions indicates either a lack of interest, a lack of critical thinking skills, or a lack of engagement, none of which are ideal to end an interview with.

A couple of other considerations that are worthy of mention include environmental observation and mirroring. When you enter a person's office, notice their surroundings. Are there family pictures or sports memorabilia displayed? Are there books about certain topics on their bookcase shelves? This will help you get to know who you are talking to and allows you the opportunity to learn more about the person...note, always keep it professional. People love to talk about themselves so encourage them to do so.

There is an NLP (Neuro-Linguistic Programming) technique of mirroring that is also worthy of mentioning. Be aware of the language style, mannerisms, and posture of the interviewer. People are usually most comfortable talking when the person they are talking to is exhibiting a similar posture, tone, and presence. In the same way, it is most comfortable to be standing if the person you are talking to is standing, or sitting at a similar height if both of you are sitting, mimicking the interviewer's posture can put them, and you, more at ease. If the interviewer is leaning in, lean in. If the interviewer is more relaxed or crosses their legs, go ahead and assume a more relaxed stance and cross your legs (unless you are considered royalty, and then you are only supposed to cross your ankles). This can be relatively easily done and tastefully accomplished if you expand your awareness. Consider your posture in all modalities of interviewing be it phone, video, or face-to-face.

Panel or Multi-Person Interviews

A panel or multi-person interview is when there is more than one company interviewer. This allows the company to see how you react in a more meeting-style environment. Each company interviewer will have their own goals in understanding a candidate's fit. It might include your potential direct supervisor or co-workers, HR representatives, or people from outside the department from which you are seeking employment. They want to evaluate multiple characteristics about you. The advantage for you is the opportunity to impress multiple people at the same time. It is still important to ask good questions. You also can gain a wider perspective on the culture and environment you will possibly be entering.

It is important to be aware of the interviewers and what backgrounds they have. Hopefully, you were able to ascertain the names and positions of those who you will be talking to before showing up at the company and have already done your research on their backgrounds. This is consistent with the prepared conversation above. LinkedIn is a golden tool for that type of research. Networking will also help you to be able to ask people in your network what they know about those that will be interviewing you.

They Get to Know You

This type of interview is usually much less formal and can take place at networking events in the community or at the company. This also happens at job fairs. In this arena, you still need to be prepared with questions and have done your homework. When you go to a job fair, for example, you will want to have examined a list of organizations participating, select a few to specifically target, and do your homework. You also want to be open to exploring companies that you may not have specifically researched while you are there.

Stress Placed in the Interview

Many times, the job interview encompasses questions that are scenario based. Questions are asked to gauge your response to stressful situations. This is especially prevalent in potentially high-stress roles so that you can be evaluated on how you work under pressure. You might think the interview itself is pressure enough, but if you work at a 911 center or in many healthcare-related positions, you need to be able to deal with high-stress situations. The key to succeeding is staying calm and thoughtful through the process. Take a deep breath if you need to redirect some of that stress.

Case Interviews

You are provided with a project or scenario and need to come up with an appropriate response or solution. These are designed to test your problem-solving skills and thought process. Problems could be real or fictional situations. The best preparation for these types of interviews, and interviews in general, is having adequate sleep. No, we're not talking about sleeping at the interview, but being well-rested before participating in the interview. Programmers may be given a program to develop. Marketers might need to design a campaign.

Structured vs Unstructured

A structured interview has specific questions that are asked of all candidates. Unstructured interviews are a bit more free-flowing and follow the conversation in whichever direction it flows. Whichever direction, you need to be prepared to answer all types of questions. Practice is the best preparation to help you shine.

Types of Questions

Questions can come in many forms. You might get behavioral questions that ask you how you have reacted in the past in certain situations. You want to have a pool of stories to share. You might be asked purely factual-type questions for which you want to be able to be well-versed in the facts. You might be asked what you might consider strange questions like if you were a tree, what kind of tree would you be? Such questions may sound silly, but they do demonstrate how you think on your feet. All questions are designed to probe who you are and why they should hire you.

Make sure to answer all questions honestly and with spirit. As in public speaking, you want to be expressive by varying tones, pace, and volume, while also using appropriate hand gestures to express your responses. It is also okay to delay answering a question by commenting something like "Excellent question, let me think that through for a minute" or repeat the question back to the interviewer to not only verify you got it right but to also give you additional time to consider your answer. You can then ask for clarification on a question to determine what is really being asked.

Answering and Asking Questions

Remember, this period of inquisition is two-sided.

2 Ears - 1 Mouth

During the interview session, remember we were given 2 ears and 1 mouth. This means we listen twice as much as we speak.

Dress for Success

Make sure to dress well for the interview. Dress a little above the team apparel. You will know what the team wears by asking before you interview and seeing them on the website and on LinkedIn.

CAR Method

This is the best way to respond to a behavioral question when asked. Based on the STAR method of situation, task at the time, action taken, and results, as previously discussed in this book, the CAR method is a little more streamlined and starts with the challenge. It then calls for your sharing of the action and the results. These types of questions demonstrate how you respond to situations and your capacity, ability, and aptitude for learning and growing. It provides the employer with a snapshot of how you handle stressful situations, problem-solve, and work as a team player.

Here is an example of an interview question that is responded to using CAR.

Question: Describe what happens when you help a difficult customer.

Answer: I was working online as a customer service representative in the ordering department taking care of a customer who was very angry that her Christmas present arrived three days after Christmas. I listened carefully and gave her all the time and space needed for her to vent her anger. When she was finished, I apologized and offered to send her a voucher for her to receive a free item up to the cost of the gift item. She agreed. Before the call ended, I again apologized, and the caller was calmer and satisfied.

Can you see in this answer how an employer sees calmness in a stressful situation, compassion, taking responsibility, and working within the parameters to take care of the needs of a customer? Of course, this answer will score points on the interview sheet!

Stay Curious

Always wanting to learn more is the attitude that conveys your aptitude for growing.

What's legal to ask (them and you)

In the same way you typically don't include marital status, family information, or other personal demographic information on your resume or LinkedIn profile, many of the questions related to religion, sex, age, or others of a personal nature are illegal. That doesn't mean they don't get asked, and although you never want to attack your interviewer for asking such questions, a bad idea, you can politely decline. Sometimes interviewers test you to see how far they can go before getting pushback or are purposely adding stress to test how you would react. Other times they are just not knowledgeable in the law. Be careful, but feel free to share what you feel comfortable with.

Follow Up

Make sure to write thank you notes to EVERYBODY you talk to. This is not optional. You want to stand out and be top of mind when the question is being asked at the company "So who should we hire". Every chance you get to impress, from dress, to enthusiasm, to radiating positivity, you can gain the edge in being chosen. Thank you notes indicate courtesy and further allow for follow-up regarding qualifications, things forgotten to be said or asked in the interview, or a way to demonstrate communication skills. Such letters must be grammatically perfect (thank you www.grammarly.com). It is also a nice gesture to give a little extra by possibly including an article or link to a resource that the person you had spoken with might appreciate. You might have heard the expression under promise and over deliver, well this falls into the over-deliver category with the recipient getting a pleasant surprise that may help them in their roles.

Attitude

While interviewing, take the perspective that you already have the job. This will lend confidence and a positive bearing to your interactions and answers during the interview.

You've got this!

Chapter Summary

- There are many different forms of interviews, but preparation and practice is key.

- Ensuring you capture the moment and impress the interviewers is what total preparation does.

- Be sure to know the most recent news of the company and bring this up in the question-and-answer portion of the interview. Phrase a futuristic question surrounding the news item.
- Be ready to ask questions that paint the picture of you working with them.
- Interview with confidence.

>>> (Optional) You can go to the online course workbook. and complete the exercise: The STAR chart and the Interview Prep

chart. This is part of the online course Module 11 Kill the Interview Assignment and Exercise.

The Question:

How do I best get the interview skills I need to succeed when interviewing and what do I need to remember to not do?

The AI Response:

1. Research: Research the company, the job description and the interviewer to ensure you are adequately prepared for the interview.

2. Practice: Practice your answers to potential questions and rehearse them with a friend.

3. Body Language: Speak confidently, make eye contact, and maintain an open posture.

4. Listen: Listen carefully to the interviewer and answer questions directly and honestly.

5. Ask Questions: Ask questions about the job, the company, and the interviewer.

6. Follow Up: Follow up with a thank-you note or email after the interview.

7. Don't: Don't be overly aggressive, don't lie, and don't speak negatively about past employers.

Author's Comment on AI Response:

Good reminders, especially the practice, practice, practice. You might even want to go on interviews for opportunities you might not have a lot of interest in to get the practice. Not only might you get more comfortable with the process, but while interviewing, the potential employer might say "Actually, you could probably be very effective in this role (or not), but we do have another opportunity that might even be a better fit for your skills and abilities. Any interest?" Also, as previously mentioned in the chapter, don't forget the power of a good night's sleep and being early, though not too early, to the interview. Also remember, what you say in the interview is likely to be remembered when you get hired, so always be honest.

12 EVALUATING AND ACCEPTING THE JOB OFFER

Making choices and negotiating success.

What this chapter covers:

- Deciding (having multiple offers).

- Negotiation (this may be uncomfortable for some people).

- Salaries, moving/relocation expenses, benefits, workspace, technology, etc.

- Accepting gleefully, declining gracefully.

- Ask about mentorship and onboarding.

The day has arrived you have worked very hard to have. You got an email, text, or a phone call telling you that the employer has selected you for the career position. But the day gets better. You receive more than one of these messages, and now you must decide as to where you want to contribute with compensation.

Deciding with Multiple Offers

It can feel overwhelming to have more than one employer want to hire you. Look at this as an opportunity to be where you want to be, and where you will fit best, long-term.

This is the whole point of this book and course: you get to be where you want to be, and contribute to maximum benefit, and not where you are just needing to be employed!

So, how do you decide?

Look to see one more time their culture, mission, and team members. Now you are looking at this from the perspective of "Do I really want to be there?" Before, as a job candidate, you were looking at this as a possibility for the future. Now, with a different perspective and different lens, you are asking yourself, "Will I be happy being here and make a difference?"

Keep in mind that if you are contributing with compensation, typically for 40+ hours per week. You are likely there more than you are anywhere else.

Typically, in a single day of 24 hours:

We sleep 8 hours.

We work 8 hours.

We commute (up to 2 hours)

We exercise 1-2 hours.

We interact with friends and family or watch TV for up to 4 hours.

You see? You are with your team contributing with compensation more of the hours of the day than being at home. You need to be happy where you contribute with compensation.

Negotiation

Especially in cases where you have more than one employer offering you the position, you have the leverage to bargain for your contribution to the success of their team.

Salaries

Salaries are one part of a compensation package. Up for negotiation are a multitude of factors including educational opportunities (paid), workspace tools (tech tools to help you do your job better), flextime, and work-from-home vs. in-office requirements. Moving expense reimbursement. Now is the time to negotiate for specific growth opportunities, conference participation, certification support, or other things that will enhance your value to the organization as well as your professional development.

Accepting

Accepting the role and compensation package is exciting to all engaged in the process. Having clear expectations as to work schedule and being able to meet personal commitments (planned vacations or important family events) should also be discussed before final acceptance.

Mentorship and Onboarding

Having received the offer, and negotiated critical aspects as to responsibilities and expectations, you want to set yourself up for long-term success. You will likely want to discuss mentorship opportunities where you can be matched up with an existing staff member that is familiar with the organization. If there is no formal mentorship program, you still want to ask about the possibility of being assigned a mentor.

Additionally, you may want to negotiate for two things related to your next review. Timing and expectations. As part of the negotiation, you may find they have an annual review process which is normally your next opportunity for a raise. You may try and request to push up that timetable and seek a 3-month or 6-month review with the potential for promotion.

Another powerful question to ask is for the official form that will be used to evaluate your performance. Knowing what they will be evaluating you on at the time of your will give you additional insight into expectations and how your contributions will be examined. You can go through these reviews prepared to demonstrate your ability to meet their desired criteria of success.

>>> (Optional) You can go to the online course workbook. and complete the exercise: Contemplating job acceptance checklist. This is part of an online Module 12 Contemplating a Job Offer Exercise.

Chapter Summary

- You are at work for most of your life so be sure you are happy where you work.

- You have the power to negotiate, to some extent, as you are in the process of accepting the job offer.

The Question:

I got the job, how do I best negotiate to improve the offer and what are the top 10 sites, with URLs, that can help me do the research?

The AI Response:

1. Do your research. Before entering into a negotiation, it's important to know the market value of the position you're applying for, as well as the range of salaries and benefits offered by the employer.

2. Present your qualifications and experience. Show the employer why you are a valuable asset to the company and why you deserve a higher salary and better benefits.

3. Make reasonable requests. Demonstrate why you deserve an increase in salary or benefits, and make reasonable requests that are feasible for the employer.

4. Be prepared to compromise. Be open to compromise and be willing to negotiate with the employer to find a mutually beneficial agreement.

5. Remain professional and polite. Negotiating is a delicate matter, so it's important to remain professional and polite at all times.

Top 10 sites:

1. Glassdoor: https://www.glassdoor.com/

2. Salary.com: https://www.salary.com/

3. PayScale: https://www.payscale.com/

4. Indeed Salary: https://www.indeed.com/salary

5. Robert Half Salary Guide: https://www.roberthalf.com/salary-guide

6. Bureau of Labor Statistics: https://www.bls.gov/

7. Monster.com Salary & Benefits: https://hiring.monster.com/employer-resources/compensation-benefits/

8. WorldatWork: https://www.worldatwork.org/

9. The Riley Guide: http://www.rileyguide.com/salary.html

10. National Association of Colleges & Employers: https://www.naceweb.org/

When negotiating the offer, there are a few key points to keep in mind. First, prepare yourself with research on comparable salaries, job titles, and industry trends. Have an idea of your bottom line and what you are willing to accept. Make sure you are confident in the value you bring to the company and how your skills fit their needs. Listen carefully to the employer and understand their point of view and motivations. Consider their full offer, which could include benefits, bonuses, and performance incentives. Be sure to get the details of the offer in writing before you accept. Finally, be flexible and remain professional throughout the process.

Author's Comment on AI Response:

As part of your company research, you want to make sure to be aware of the salaries and benefits. Make sure they align with your needs and desires. Also remember, you are negotiating a total package. Employers will often be more open to one-time adjustments such as a sign-on bonus, moving expenses, and giving you tech to better do your job rather than increasing the salary. You may also want to consider HSAs (Health Savings Accounts) rather than a specific medical plan if you are younger and/or in pretty good health. There are many advantages to HSAs, especially given the fact they allow you to keep what you don't spend. Use your soft skills well when negotiating.

13 SUCCESS [SO-CALLED SOFT] SKILLS

Keys to lifetime career growth and personal success.

"Live as if you were to die tomorrow. Learn as if you were to live forever."

Mahatma Gandhi

What this chapter covers:

- What are they and why do you need them?
- Building and developing YOUR skills.
- What employers want: NACE Competencies.
- Skill gaps.

- 16 Quotient Query: Intelligence, Emotional, Cultural, Adversity, Growth, Potential, Relational, Spiritual, You, Why, Adaptability, Digital, Creativity, Failure, Crisis, Leadership quotients **IQ-EQ-CQ-AQ-GQ-PQ-RQ-SQ-UQ-YQ-AQ2-DQ-CQ2-FQ-CQ3-LQ.**

- Additional Skills include Business Interpersonal Communication, Conflict-Negotiation, Time management, Stress Management, Money/budget management, Teamwork, Public Speaking, Writing, Taking Initiative, Networking, Attitude, Resilience, Ethics, and Integrity.

- Invest in YOURSELF - TAKE INITIATIVE.

- Overcoming "Imposter Syndrome."

Why You Need So-Called "Soft Skills?"

Success in a career is intentional and not accidental. This means that just like in a personal relationship when working at the relationship makes it grow and be sustainable, so does a professional career. You must put in the time and effort toward succeeding in your career. You do this by exercising and implementing "soft skills."

What Are These Soft Skills?

Here is a list of many of them (this is not an exhaustive list):

- Active listening.

- Effectively communicating (written and oral).

- Compassionate perspective.

- Patient understanding.

- Positivity

- Integrity

- Human-to-human interaction with no judgment.

- No stereotyping, no generalizing, no causal attribution.

- Believe in the best of people.
- Take responsibility for your actions.
- Make your boss look great.

This is only a partial listing of soft skills that help you succeed.

If you wish to learn about these skills in more depth, take our next course in Life Skills

Developing And Maintaining Your Skills

The best way to succeed in your personal and professional life is to learn and practice these skills daily.

What skills employers want you to have

There was a study conducted and reported by the National Association of Colleges and Employers (NACE) that we listed in Chapter 3 and are listing again in this chapter.

Problem-solving	**Strong work ethic**
Analytical/quantitative	**Technical**
Ability to work in a team	**Flexibility/Adaptability**
Communication (written and oral)	**Detail-oriented**
Initiative	**Leadership**
Interpersonal (relates well with other people)	

Looking at this list, you can sense that by learning these skills and using them, you can succeed in both your professional and personal life.

The point of this book and course is to prepare you for a career where you are doing what you love and love what you do in the team where you want to be learning, growing, and sharing yourself while continually being challenged and succeeding. We noticed there are additional skills that help a person make it through tough times while on the job or at home. These skills are what we call "the 18 Q's.

"IQ-EQ-CQ-AQ-GQ-PQ-RQ-SQ-UQ-YQ-AQ2-DQ-CQ2-FQ-CQ3-LQ-PQ-SQ"

*Intelligence quotient (IQ)

*Emotional quotient (EQ)

*Cultural quotient (CQ)

*Adversity quotient (AQ)

Growth quotient (GQ)

Potential quotient (PQ)

Relational quotient (RQ)

Spiritual quotient (SQ)

You Quotient (YQ)

Why Quotient (YQ)

Adaptability Quotient (AQ2)

Digital Quotient (DQ)

Creativity Quotient (CQ2)

Failure Quotient (FQ)

Crisis Quotient (CQ3)

Leadership Quotient (LQ)

Positive Quotient (PQ)

Social Quotient (SQ)

*We bring these quotients to your attention because when operating with high levels of these quotients, you are most assuredly successful in your personal and professional life.

For the time being, we are focusing on the first four quotients. To get more information about the other 14 quotients, what they are, how they are measured, and how you can raise your score, stay tuned for future mini courses from *Future Forward Academy*.

IQ=Intelligence Quotient — Measure of Intelligence

The intelligence quotient (IQ) used to be the measure of one's capability and ability for the altitude of their aptitude determining the career course of action. Historically, it was invented in France in 1905 to determine which students needed additional attention to help them learn. It was used by the military in the early 1900s to determine which of the recruits were suited for leadership positions.[1]

Based on this measure, it was determined whether a person can contribute to their own defense at trial, secure benefits in the form of social security, identify learning disabilities, if certain therapy or medical treatment impacts cognitive function, and, help advance the artificial intelligence (AI) in computer systems.

There is a lot of controversy regarding the use of IQ testing. Some say it is biased against those who, through no fault of their own, did not get the same level of education as others or those who grew up in a culture that did not promote learning. For this book and course, our emphasis is more on the other quotients rather than the intelligence quotient.

Eq-Emotional Quotient — Measure Of Emotional Intelligence

There are a greater number of employers requiring their job candidates to have emotional intelligence training and experience. The reason for this is that social scientists found that people with high levels of emotional intelligence are most likely to be resilient, retained, and responsible. These are three very important qualities of an employee to an employer.

Emotional Intelligence (EQ) greatly influences our reasoning, interactions, decisions, projects, relationships, and other areas, while carrying distinct outcomes and requiring distinct practices to build. When this skill is activated, interactions between employers and employees go more smoothly. Interactions between co-workers take place more peacefully, and customer/client interactions with employees take place in a more positive, civil, and tranquil environment.

What exactly is Emotional Intelligence? Emotional intelligence is **the ability to identify and regulate one's emotions and understand the emotions of others**. A high EQ helps you to build relationships, reduce team stress, defuse conflicts, and improve job satisfaction.[2]

Simply put, it is knowing when to say something versus when to be quiet and still. It is knowing when to step into a situation and work to affect the outcome, and when to step aside. When acting with emotional intelligence, you read the room and know intuitively how to respond to a situation.

According to Dr. Daniel Goleman, a leading psychologist in the field of emotional intelligence and the author of *Emotional Intelligence: Why it can matter more than IQ,* there are five pillars of emotional intelligence.[2]

- Self-Awareness: the ability to see one's own emotions, and know one's emotional triggers, strengths, weaknesses, motivations, values, core beliefs, aspirations, and goals while understanding and appreciating how these affect one's thoughts and behaviors.

- Self-Management: the ability to regulate and manage one's emotions, behaviors, and motivations as it applies to any given situation. Essentially controlling emotions and not letting emotions control you.

- Motivation: the ability to take action consistent with the force that prompts us such as aspirations, goals, and dreams.

- Empathy: the ability to connect emotionally with others while considering their feelings, opinions, beliefs, and perspectives; positively responding to the emotional needs of others.

- Relationship Management: the ability to build and maintain genuine trust, respect, rapport, and confidence from others.

>(Optional) You can go to the online course workbook. and complete the exercise: Emotional Intelligence diagnosis survey. This is part of an online course Module 13 Emotional Intelligence Exercise.

Now you can see how this skill helps a person be successful. When all five pillars are in operation in one's life, you are likely to meet with personal and professional success. Another skill that addresses interactions related to the Emotional Quotient is the Cultural Quotient.

CQ-Cultural Quotient — Measure of Cultural Intelligence

Cultural intelligence is very important to your continued career success, especially in this age of DEI & B (Diversity, Equity, Inclusion, and Belonging) awareness. The definition of cultural intelligence is *"an outsider's seemingly natural ability to interpret someone's unfamiliar and ambiguous gestures the way that a person's compatriots would."* People with high cultural intelligence are **attuned to the values, beliefs, and styles of communication of people from different cultures**. They use this knowledge to help them relate to others with empathy and understanding.[3]

Cultural intelligence is related to emotional intelligence, but it picks up where emotional intelligence leaves off. A person with high emotional intelligence grasps what makes us human and at the same time what makes each of us different from one another.[3] It is recognizing the human aspects of interacting and responding to others. Emotions, attitudes, beliefs, opinions of a person with diverse backgrounds, and ethnicities are responded to with dignity, value, and validation by a person with a high level of cultural intelligence.

According to the CQ Model, there are four dimensions of Cultural Intelligence.[4]

CQ Drive is the willingness to work with others from diverse backgrounds. It includes an ability to overcome explicit or unconscious bias and the capacity to persist in challenging intercultural settings—even when the individual feels confused, frustrated, or burnt out. CQ Drive is the extent to which one is energized and persistent in one's approach to multicultural situations, one's self-efficacy, and sense of deriving benefit from intercultural interactions.

CQ Knowledge is an understanding of culture, cultural differences, and similarities. CQ knowledge is the degree to which one understands how culture, cultural scripts, and systems influence how people think and behave.

CQ Strategy is the ability to adapt mentally. With high CQ Strategy, individuals understand that the cultural dimensions that constitute worldviews are multiple and likely different to one's own, and awareness of these assists in the development of strategies for interpersonal and community relations and business success.

CQ Action is the extent to which you can act appropriately in multicultural situations. It includes one's flexibility to adapt verbal and non-verbal behaviors and to adapt to different cultural norms to intentionally improve the relationship or interaction. CQ Action decreases the risk of miscommunication and helps an individual respond to diverse others in a manner that conveys respect and builds trust and rapport.

If you are reading this and realize you may need to improve your cultural quotient, you are not alone.

There is a way to measure the strength of your cultural intelligence and improve upon it.

>>>(Optional) You can go to the online course workbook. and complete the exercise: Cultural Intelligence diagnosis survey and engage in our exercises to strengthen emotional and cultural intelligences. This is part of an online course Module 13 Exercise: Cultural Intelligence.

The next quotient that impacts the potential of one's career success is the Adversity Quotient (AQ).

AQ–Adversity Quotient —measure of ability to respond to adversity

This is a measure of a person's ability to bounce back from a setback in life or on the job. We all periodically experience setbacks. How we respond to those setbacks can be a major factor in how we attain long-term success. Adversity is defined as the ability of an individual to think, manage, direct, and endure challenges and difficulties in life.[2] Dr. Paul Stoltz was the one who proposed the concept of AQ and used this measure to categorize people into three categories: "Quitters," "Campers," and "Climbers."[5]

Quitters are easily broken by negative events and become hopeless about their success; live compromised and miserable lives.[2]

Campers are ready to fight and are not persistent in their efforts; prefer a comfortable life and any negative experience makes them scared; only happy if their life flows smoothly.[5]

Climbers are the real achievers; ready to fight to attain success regardless of the challenge they face; never give up achieving their goal; nothing in life can defeat them; self-motivated and consistent with their efforts; highly optimistic and never lose hope.

Which of these categories do you fit (at this time)?

Dr. Stoltz gave us a way to measure ourselves using CORE.

- Control– It is the extent to which individuals can manage their life and control the negative consequences before getting worse.

- Ownership– It is the extent to which you are accountable for your actions and are willing to take responsibility to make adverse situations better.

- Reach– It is the extent to which the challenges you face extrapolate to other aspects of your life. It measures how capable you are of resisting such challenges from affecting other necessities such as your profession or family life.

- Endurance– It is the extent to which you are capable of tolerating pain and yet being optimistic about the future and believing that something positive waits for you on the opposite side of all adversities.

If you are not a "Climber," then there is some work to be done for you to become one.

Employers want their employees to have resistance to negative circumstances and maintain hope, and not give up. According to Elizabeth Le Thi (2007), quitters are less ambitious and never take up any complex responsibilities, campers are willing to put in a minimal amount of effort, and climbers are the ideal workforce since they are highly motivated and committed to grow and excel in life.[3]

Rest assured, there is a way to convert your adversity response tendencies and raise your adversity quotient. The method is proposed by Dr. Stoltz as being LEAD.

Stoltz formulated the LEAD sequence which consists of the following four guidelines:[2]

- Listen to your response to adversity.

- Establish accountability.

- Analyze the evidence.

- Do something.

>>> (Optional) You can go to the online course workbook. and complete the exercise: Adversity Intelligence diagnosis survey. This is part of an online course Module 13 Adversity Quotient Exercise.

Which category of adversity actors are you?

Now you can get a sense of why it is important to your success that you become a Climber when it comes to responding to adversity.

Imposter Syndrome

What is imposter syndrome and how does that affect your career success?

Simply put, this syndrome is the feeling you do not belong or deserve to be in the position you are holding. This phenomenon is detrimental to your continued career success and happiness in many other areas of your life.

Types of Imposter Syndrome

Imposter syndrome can be broken down into five basic types:

- The Perfectionist. This type of imposter syndrome involves believing that, unless you were perfect, you could have done better. You feel like an imposter because your perfectionist traits make you believe that you're not as good as others might think you are.

- The Expert. The expert feels like an imposter because they don't know everything there is to know about a particular subject or topic, or they haven't mastered every step in a process. Because there is more for them to learn, they don't feel as if they've reached the rank of "expert."

- The Natural Genius. In this imposter syndrome type, you may feel like a fraud simply because you don't believe that you are naturally intelligent or competent. If you don't get something right the first time around or it takes you longer to master a skill, you feel like an imposter.

- The Soloist. It's also possible to feel like an imposter if you had to ask for help to reach a certain level or status. Since you couldn't get there on your own, you question your competence or abilities.

- The Superperson. This type of imposter syndrome involves believing that you must be the hardest worker or reach the highest levels of achievement possible and, if you don't, you are a fraud.

-

Impact of Imposter Syndrome

For some people, impostor syndrome can fuel motivation to achieve, but this usually comes at the cost of experiencing constant anxiety. You might over-prepare or work much harder than necessary, for instance, to "make sure" nobody finds out you are a fraud. Eventually, anxiety worsens and may lead to depression.

This sets up a vicious cycle, in which you think that the only reason you survived that class presentation was that you stayed up all night rehearsing. Or you think the only reason you got through that party or family gathering was that you memorized details about all the guests so you would always have ideas for small talk.

There are signs, symptoms, and solutions to this syndrome.

Signs of Imposter Syndrome

Some common characteristics of imposter syndrome include:

- An inability to realistically assess your competence and skills.

- Attributing your success to external factors.

- Berating your performance

- Fear that you won't live up to expectations.

- Overachieving

- Sabotaging your own success

- Setting very challenging goals and feeling disappointed when you fall short.

Symptoms: If you wonder whether you might have imposter syndrome, ask yourself the following questions:

- Do you agonize over even the smallest mistakes or flaws in your work?

- Do you attribute your success to luck or outside factors?

- Are you sensitive to even constructive criticism?

- Do you feel like you will inevitably be found out as a phony?

- Do you downplay your own expertise, even in areas where you are genuinely more skilled than others?

Possible Solutions to Imposter Syndrome

To move past these feelings, you need to become comfortable confronting some of the deeply ingrained beliefs you hold about yourself. This exercise can be hard because you might not even realize that you hold them, but here are some techniques you can use:[8]

- Share your feelings. Talk to other people about how you are feeling. Irrational beliefs tend to fester when they are hidden and not talked about.

- Focus on others. While this might feel counterintuitive, try to help others In the same situation as you. If you see someone who seems awkward or alone, ask them a question to bring them into the group. As you practice your skills, you will build confidence in your abilities.

- Assess your abilities. If you have long-held beliefs about your incompetence in social and performance situations, make a realistic assessment of your abilities. Write down your accomplishments and what you are good at, then compare these with your self-assessment.

- Take baby steps. Don't focus on doing things perfectly, but rather, do things reasonably well and reward yourself for taking action. For example, in a group conversation, offer an opinion or share a story about yourself.

- Question your thoughts. As you start to assess your abilities and take baby steps, question whether your thoughts are rational. Does it make sense to believe that you are a fraud given everything that you know?

- Stop comparing. Every time you compare yourself to others in a social situation, you will find some fault with yourself that fuels the feeling of not being good enough or not belonging. Instead, during conversations, focus on listening to what the other person is saying. Be genuinely interested in learning more.

- Use social media moderately. We know that the overuse of social media may be related to feelings of inferiority. If you try to portray an image on social media that doesn't match who you really are or that is impossible to achieve, it will only make your feelings of being a fraud worse.

- Stop fighting your feelings. Don't fight the feelings of not belonging. Instead, try to lean into them and accept them. It's only when you acknowledge these feelings that you can start to unravel the core beliefs that are holding you back.

- Refuse to let it hold you back. No matter how much you feel like you are a fraud or that you don't belong, don't let that stop you from pursuing your goals. Keep going and refuse to be stopped.

In addition to these exercises, as prescribed in the article, it is best to gather remnants of your time and effort in the form of an e-portfolio. This prevents you from having imposter syndrome. You see for yourself what you can do based on what you have already accomplished! □

Create an e-portolio. The process of creating this portfolio allows you to see for yourself what you have accomplished.

Feel proud of these accomplishments and look forward to making many more accomplishments in the future.

>>>>>> (Optional) You can go to the online course workbook. and do the exercise creating an e-portfolio This is part of an online course Module 13 – Creating an E-Portfolio.<<<<<

----

[1]https://www.verywellmind.com/history-of-intelligence-testing-2795581

[2]https://www.latrobe.edu.au/nest/why-emotional-intelligence-makes-you-more-successful/#:~:text=Emotional%20intelligence%20is%20the%20ability,conflict%20and%20improve%20job%20satisfaction.

[3]https://hbr.org/2004/10/cultural-intelligence

[4]https://theewgroup.com/us/blog/what-is-cultural-intelligence/

[5]http://www.thecqmodel.com/

[6]https://www.psychologs.com/article/how-does-adversity-quotient-define-ones-ability-to-endure

[7]Thi, E.L. (2007). Adversity quotient in predicting job performance viewed through the perspective of the big five. https://core.ac.uk/download/pdf/30860559.pdf

[8]https://www.verywellmind.com/imposter-syndrome-and-social-anxiety-disorder-4156469

Chapter Summary

- The skills it takes to have rousing and continual career success are immense and important.

- It takes time to learn, build, and master the skills employers want you to have, so be diligent and patient.

- Knowing your quotient measures gives you an idea as to how successful you can become and what you can do to improve yourself for greater success.

The Question:

What are the top 20 soft skills desired by an employer and how might I best get them?

The AI Response:

1. Communication Skills

2. Problem-Solving Skills

3. Interpersonal Skills

4. Teamwork Skills

5. Leadership Skills

6. Adaptability

7. Conflict Resolution

8. Time Management

9. Critical Thinking

10. Decision Making

11. Negotiation

12. Self-Motivation

13. Public Speaking

14. Emotional Intelligence

15. Networking

16. Organization

17. Creativity

18. Customer Service

19. Stress Management

20. Collaboration

The best way to acquire these skills is to gain experience in related fields and practice what you learn. Take courses or attend workshops to develop and refine your skills. Participate in volunteer or internship opportunities, and actively seek out mentors to learn from. Networking, reading books and articles, and attending conferences and seminars are also great ways to build up your soft skills.

Author's Comment on AI Response:

Yes, doing your homework, practicing, and engaging are the keys to improvements in your EQ, which will carry you far in your personal and professional life. Whether it's professional associations, hobby groups, or church groups, you want to build a deep foundation in these skills. As previously mentioned, www.Toasmasters.org can help you with many of the ChatGPT skills mentioned, especially if you take on a leadership role - and it's a great resume/LinkedIn stuffer. A colleague of mine, the number 2 person at a major manufacturer shared that he could always tell if the interview candidate had been in Toastmasters. He said, "They are more engaging, well poised, able to think on their feet and hold an intelligent conversation, have more creativity as they answer questions...and they include it on their resume". When I commented that the resume can be the dead giveaway, he indicated that even if not included, he found those with Toastmasters experience to be better interviewees overall.

14 LIFE AND CAREER SUCCESS

"Life is a marathon, not a sprint".

"The illiterate of the 21st century will not be those who cannot read and write, but those who cannon learn, unlearn, and relearn."

Alvin Toffler, Author of Future Shock (1970)

You might be stunned, in shock, and feeling greatly overwhelmed when you see the previously mentioned list of soft skills. After all, we just listed for you many skills in the previous chapter, and you are probably thinking "Enough already." Di I need all these skills to be successful in life?

The answer is YES.

It takes a great many skills working in tandem for someone to have a successful life. Every moment of every day presents challenges and opportunities. These challenges are met with these skills in this chapter and the skills presented in the previous chapter. Sometimes, you are using a combination of these skills much in the same way a surgeon uses different instruments, or a carpenter uses different construction and fixing tools.

Three relationships that make or break our lives:

- Spiritual connection/relationship

- Human connection/relationship

- Relationship with money

If any of these relationships are out of whack, you are affected in ways you may not be aware of. The content of this chapter is meant to help you establish and maintain these relationships and have a great life.

You are probably reading this because you are at a point in life where you are removing or transplanting something in your life or wanting and needing to build or fix something in your life. If this is the case, you are in the right place. Keep reading.

What this chapter covers:

- Having a spiritual connection.
- Business Interpersonal communication.
- It's NOT about you, and it's NOT personal – careful about the emotions and reactions.
- Life-long learning/Upskilling/Certifications/Micro-Credentials.
- Gap analysis
- Taking Charge of YOUR Future.
- Conflict-negotiation
- Reliability/dependability
- Time management
- Stress management
- Hobbies
- Storytelling 101
- LISTENING skills – 2 ears, 1-mouth (heard that before)
- Follow up and follow through!
- You Don't know it all...ASK FOR HELP, the law of reciprocity.
- Money/Budget management
- Family/Friends Relationships considerations
- Giving back

Attitude/Whatever it Takes/YOUR priorities/Sell yourself every day/create "flow"/Master conflict turn into productive/build your portfolio of reports.

Having a Spiritual Connection

Human beings are spirit beings. Not sure this is true? Think about what you do when encountering something bigger than what you can handle, such as major illness, personal distress, financial worries, mental anguish, facing life or death situations. Whatever the case, most people instinctively pray or talk to the deity they trust. Having a healthy spiritual connection is what can make the difference between living a life with faith or one full of fear. People having a life with faith also have hope that provides energy for positivity. People not having faith, instead of fear that debilitates and suffocates life and energy for the future.

In essence, the best way forward is to have some spiritual connection to have a life of faith and not fear. With faith, all things are possible due to its positive energy. Positivity breeds positivity and positive outcomes for you and others in your life and work circles. Being a positive versus a negative person is the type of person most people can relate better with and want to have around. For success in life and your career, it is highly recommended that you be a person of faith and live with positivity. That way your relationships in life and work will always be positive and fruitful ones.

Business Interpersonal Communication

Business interpersonal communication is the act of writing and speaking to someone on the job. It is a skill that will save you from embarrassing moments while on the job and at home.

Speaking or writing to someone on the job is not the same as when writing to a friend or family member. Communicating with someone on the job, such as your boss or co-worker, takes a more formal approach. The words and phrasing you use are not the same words and phrases you speak and use to family and friends. The format by which you write follows a certain protocol to be deemed professional.

Why should it matter how you speak and write while on the job? Does it matter?

It does matter. You are representing your brand in your speech and your writing. People in professions expect certain language and phrasing. If you do not meet this expectation, your credibility as someone who is seen as competent and capable is at risk. You might not be taken seriously and as a result, miss out on something that could enhance your career. You might be laughed at or made fun of if you do not write or speak as a professional. So, here is a list of Do's and Don'ts to follow when engaged in business communication.

Do

Make sure to use the proper formatting for what you are about to write. For example, a business letter format is different from a resume format, cover letter, business proposal format, fundraising letter, thank you letter, acceptance letter, resignation letter, or letter of intent.

Use plain and clear phrasing.

Always include a call to action (when appropriate)

Write in an uplifting and positive tone. (Even in negative circumstances, there is room for positivity)

Write with a tone of respect.

Do an audience analysis and know who it is that will be reading what you write. Be mindful and use your emotional intelligence.

Have someone read what you wrote before sending it (if possible)

Use a writing and editing tool such as Grammarly to ensure proper grammar and spelling.

Don't

Never use phrases of cliches, innuendos, foul language

Never have misspelled words or bad grammar

Never go over the accepted length per the letter format

Never write a business letter using the first or second person; use the third person unless the person reading the letter has a close connection and will accept seeing words such as "I," "you", "we", "us", etc.

Speaking while on the job requires finesse and the use of emotional intelligence to be acceptable. Here are some Do's and Don'ts

Do

Speak with a smile and uplifting tone.

Look someone in the eyes when you speak to them.

Listen carefully to the person before speaking to them with a response to what they just said.

Stay positive.

Seek to understand and then be understood (Stephen R. Covey)

Don't

Use foul language.

Raise your voice.

Correct someone's attitude or behavior in the presence of others.

Roll your eyes in response to what someone says.

Crossing arms when someone is talking is a sign of disrespect — don't cross your arms.

Never tap your foot when someone is talking – this is also a sign of disrespect.

It's NOT about you… and it's NOT personal - careful about the emotions and reactions.

Using your Emotional Intelligence is making sure to always be aware that what you write and what you speak you are always on the side of **RESPECT.**

This is where having and using your Emotional Intelligence will keep you on the side of respect and help you always be on the side of respect. People want to be valued and validated and know that they matter. Failing this, we get people that are out for revenge and become violent and very dangerous.

For more information and exercises to speak and write while on the job, go to our online course. This is part of an online course Module 14 Written and Oral Communication Skills Exercises

Life-long Learning/Upskilling/Certifications/Micro-Credentials

Life at times gives us a curveball by which we reassess what we are doing with our lives. This reevaluation is a time when we may realize that we need to make a career change and pivot in our life's work. This is especially true now that it is becoming apparent, we are on the precipice of a career upheaval. For many people, their career progression comes to a halt, and they will need to seek a different career. For that to occur, they may need to get skills, reskill, or upskill to meet the requirements of the new job and career.

Gap Analysis

For example, an accounting career is converting to a data analysis type of job. AI is taking over mundane data entry though it is still a human's job to collect the data, analyze it and communicate the analysis in a way that makes sense to the decision-makers of the company or corporation. Even payroll is being taken over by AI and RPA (robotic process automation) tools. If a person is an accountant or payroll officer, they need to start strategizing, planning, and preparing for the day that their position is no longer a human-based position.

Skilling, reskilling, or upskilling is when a person takes a course or enrolls in a degree or certification training curriculum that teaches them advanced knowledge for mastery in a skill they currently do not possess. For example, it may be time for an accountant to take a course in data analysis or statistics.

Taking Charge of YOUR Future

No one else but YOU know YOUR COMPASS to YOUR Northstar. What you want to do in your lifetime is up to you.

"The bad news is **time flies**. The good news is **you**'re the **pilot**." — Michael Altshuler

Where are you headed in life? Are you happy with the direction you are going? If not, then keep reading.

Have a mindset that no matter what happens, you will put forth the time and effort it takes to get to the place, occupation, and position where you love what you do and do what you love.

This means making sure you know exactly what it is that makes you happy and fulfilled. Knowing this and acting on it is what will lead you to a job and life that fulfills you and makes you feel you are contributing <u>with</u> compensation, and not <u>for</u> compensation.

As mentioned previously, before starting the job or on the first day, request a copy of the review form that is to be used in your performance evaluation. Gaining insights as to what you are scored on when it comes to performance and promotions will help you be better prepared for the review and emphasize the value you bring to what the employer is looking for.

Conflict-Negotiation

One of the best life skills to have that ensures career success is conflict negotiation capabilities. This skill allows you to promote a "win-win" solution in any given circumstance.

For example, the greatest conflict emerging inevitably is when you want or need unscheduled time off work. In the interest of fairness and getting to a "win-win" solution it is recommended you proceed in this fashion.

In your communication with your employer, you value and validate their need for your services and contribution and you offer to swap time on the job for time off the job. In other words, if there are two hours needed on Tuesday, you offer to work two hours on another day you would normally be off work. If the employer cannot allow that, then you ask them for a solution that works better for their needs and do your best to accommodate them. Remember that you were hired for your expertise and contribution. They are depending and rely on your presence.

Reliability/Dependability

Most people think that "reliability" and "dependability" have the same meaning. This is not the case. Reliability refers to the leaning on someone to get something accomplished, and dependability is the sense of security that someone will come through to get the job done and done well.

When this distinction is understood, most people react with the understanding of the need to be present on the job. The object lesson takes place in knowing what can happen to the team when a team member that is relied upon and depended upon falters and fails to be present for the team. Imagine a human pyramid and you are on the second row relying and depending on the people in the front row to support you kneeling on the back of one of them. What happens to you and the rest of the pyramid when someone from the front row falls to the ground? In this case, you are no longer supported, and you fall to the ground too. See why it is so important not to miss work?

Time Management

If you are like most people, you have a lot going on. You may be juggling several balls in the air such as family, work, business, community, hobbies, etc., and wonder how it may be possible that none of these balls drop to the ground. Managing the time in your day, week, and month is how to ensure that all the obligations tied to each ball in life get met and fulfilled.

There are many different methods by which you can manage time. The common and most effective method is to prioritize your tasks.

For more information and exercises to help with this, go to our online training course. This is part of an online course Module 14 Time Management Workbook.

Stress Management

In a stressful situation, take a breath, exhale, and take another breath and exhale. Believe it or not, the most immediate stress reducer is our breathing. Taking a breath and slowly letting it out affects our nervous system and our brain calms itself down. Breathing is a key element in meditation practice but is also powerful when not formally meditating.

Preventing stress requires the intention and advance planning to take care of yourself. Most of the time we get stressed because our needs are not being met or we are in a low energy state and cannot solve on the spot. It's like trying to run a marathon without ever training for it. So, the best way to make it through life with less stress is to take care of yourself the best you can.

Tend to your hobbies and the things that help you relax. Do not ignore having downtime. In fact, in your time management, plan for your downtime.

If you are not sure that this is true or that it works, then think about this. When was the last time you were faced with a challenge or difficulty and met it head-on successfully after having had time to rest and relax? Now when was the last time you had to deal with something, and you were not able to because of a lack of energy and mind power? See the difference? This is why you want to be operating in life with full energy, ready to meet whatever life throws at you.

Hobbies

What is it you like to do that is not working that helps you relax? Is it playing with your kids? Is it reading a book? Is it volunteering and giving back to your community? Is it watching sports or creating something? Whatever it is, this is what gets slotted for a special time on your calendar. Why do you ask? Because this is the time for you to recharge. This is the moment in the day or week when you are calm and not stressed so that your body and mind can relax.

Storytelling 101

Most people enjoy hearing a story. That may be due to the fact most of us grew up being read stories to us by our parents. We grew used to hearing the stories read before bedtime and then we read them ourselves when we got older. As adults, we seek out stories in the form of movies, books, and plays. So, is it any wonder that to have a successful career the skill of storytelling would be needed?

Sharing a story of how you made it through something challenging is an inspiration most people would love to hear. Stories of adventures and discoveries are also ones that we enjoy.

Listening skills (2 ears, 1 mouth)

Of course, on the other side of telling stories, is listening to them. This is another one of those moments where you practice the art of "value and validate."

This means you are focusing on the other person and what they are saying with your mind and your heart. You are not allowing your mind to wander to other thoughts or be thinking of what you are going to say when the other person goes to take a breath. No, you are listening intently to what and how the person is talking about to get the meaning of what is being shared. After the person has completely expressed themself, that is when you value their message and validate the meaning of the message.

Follow up and Follow Through

Ahhh — now here is where successful people get this right. Following up on what was said or done and following through on whatever tasks are needed to accomplish the goal is what successful people do. This takes intention and discipline and is included in Time Management.

You Don't know it all...ASK FOR HELP, the law of reciprocity.

As you begin to develop more skills, knowledge, and abilities and explore career options that align with them, there will be moments when you may need to know more information regarding them. This is where you park your pride and admit you need to reach out for help.

Contacting someone who has the expertise you lack is not a sign of weakness, but rather a sign of intelligence.

Be mindful of the universe principle "What goes around, comes around." As you have received help, be a willing vessel to give help to someone who asks for it. Pay it forward, which is discussed further below.

Money/Budget Management

Now this skill makes or breaks people. What happened to your bank account at the end of the month? Can you go a month or two before reaching your credit card limit to cover groceries, gas, or other must-have items? Making money and knowing how to save and spend it will serve you well.

>>> (Optional) If you lack the knowledge and skill in how to make your money and to keep from losing money, then go to the online training course. This is part of an online course Module 14 Keep from Losing Money Exercise.

Family/Relationships considerations

Try working while worried about someone in your family. Typically, it does not go well, correct? That is why having a skill that manages your personal life successfully will spill over into managing your professional life successfully.

Want to always win an argument? How about avoiding arguments altogether?

Value and validate the one you're with!

Giving Back

Paying it forward not only helps someone get what they need, but it also makes you feel good. And remember, anything that makes you feel good helps with reducing stress in life.

Some religions say it gives you good karma to give of yourself when you pay it forward. Giving what someone may need without asking or expecting anything in return is truly giving back your good fortune. Believe it or not, but this is more than a gesture, it is a skill. The skill of giving back is to know when to be charitable. Most of the time it is the right thing to do, but sometimes it might be more harmful than good. This is why it is a skill, but when done properly, it leads to great success in life for you and others.

Attitude/Whatever it Takes/YOUR priorities/Sell yourself every day/create "flow"/Master conflict turns into productive/build your portfolio of reports.

Chapter Summary

- There are several skills that it takes to have a stress-free and more blissful life.

- Knowing and mastering these skills are needed when taking care to overcome the challenges of life.

The Question:

What are the top 25 life hacks that will help with having a happier and more successful life?

The AI Response:

1. Prioritize your time - Spend your time on things that are most important to you, and don't be afraid to say 'no' to things that won't help you reach your goals.

2. Exercise regularly - Regular exercise can increase your energy levels and help you stay motivated.

3. Make healthy eating a priority - Eating healthy foods can help you feel better, stay energized, and be more productive.

4. Take time for yourself - Make sure to take time for yourself to relax and enjoy life.

5. Get organized - Take the time to organize your space, your schedule, and your life to make sure you're making the best use of your time.

6. Make lists - Lists can help you stay on track and focus on what needs to be done.

7. Get enough sleep - Getting a good night's sleep can improve your mental and physical well-being.

8. Set goals - Setting goals can help you stay focused and motivated.

9. Get enough sunlight - Sunlight can help improve your mood and help you feel more energized.

10. Spend time with people you love - Spending time with friends and family can help reduce stress and give you a sense of belonging.

11. Learn to say 'no' - Don't be afraid to turn down invitations or requests if it doesn't fit into your schedule.

12. Set boundaries - Be clear with yourself and others about what you are and aren't willing to do.

13. Practice gratitude - Take time to appreciate the good things in life, and don't be afraid to express your gratitude to others.

14. Take time for hobbies - Spend time doing things you enjoy to help reduce stress and have fun.

15. Practice mindfulness - Mindfulness can help you stay present and focused on the present moment.

16. Seek out opportunities - Look for opportunities to learn and grow, and don't be afraid to take risks.

17. Find a mentor - Find someone who can help guide you in your personal and professional life.

18. Practice self-care - Make sure to take time for yourself to relax and recharge.

19. Take risks - Don't be afraid to take risks, as it can help you grow and develop.

20. Find your passion - Find something you're passionate about and make it a priority.

21. Network - Take the time to build relationships and network with other professionals.

22. Learn from your mistakes - Don't be afraid to make mistakes, as they can help you learn and grow.

23. Develop good habits - Developing good habits can help you stay on track and reach your goals.

24. Set realistic expectations - Make sure to set realistic expectations for yourself and others.

25. Celebrate your successes - Take the time to celebrate your successes, however small they may be.

Author's Comment on AI Response:

It is all about balance. It is okay to get lost in your work (sometimes referred to as "in the zone"), your passions, and your hobbies, but if they dominate your life to where you neglect other aspects, beware. You also don't want to forget the importance of positive social interactions which often come from engaging in a variety of opportunities and experiences.

15 ADULTING 101

Making a life, not just a living.

"Who is wise? One who learns from every man. Who is strong? One who overpowers his inclinations. Who is rich? One who is satisfied with his lot. Who is honorable, one who honors his fellows"

Shimon ben Zoma in Pirkei Avos – Ethics of the Fathers

What this chapter covers:

- Managing Credit
- Basic Budgeting - Based on your paycheck.

- Health Care/Self Care
- Time management
- Life Balance - Wheel of Life
- Finding a house/apartment
- How to do taxes
- Grocery shopping
- Insurance
- Retirement - NEVER too early...Stats
- Pay yourself first.
- Simple car maintenance
- Basic house maintenance and handling emergencies
- Entrepreneurship & the Gig Economy
- Giving back Give before you Get
- Etiquette - WFH & Office
- Ethical Behavior/Decision Making!
- It's not all Black & White...**It Depends**
- DE&I, ESG, CSR
- Brainstorming Techniques
- Engaging in LIFE

Being an adult means that you are ready to cover your costs, take responsibility for your actions or inactions, and live with the consequences. You are also making choices that make the most sense for your life, morally and ethically.

Taking the time to think, rethink and reflect takes maturity too. This is the opposite of impulse buying and acting on impulse, most especially when deciding on a purchase involving credit.

Managing Credit

Buy now, pay later ... it's a trap! Most people just want the merchandise now and deal with the monthly payment. All that is asked is "How much is the monthly payment?" But wait a minute, please. Think about the cost of the merchandise after all the payments are made.

See this illustration.

Cost of Credit

Paying off your credit card balance late can increase interest an unexpected costs. Learn how much more you might pay on pur due to the cost of credit.

Total purchase amount
This is how much you charge to your credit card

567

Credit card APR
This is the annual interest rate charged by your credit card

23

Planned monthly payment
This is how much you intend to pay each month to pay off your credit card bill

12

Results

Number of months to pay off	125
This is how long it will take you to pay off the entire amount.	
Final month's payment	$3.98
The last payment on this account	
Total finance charge	$924.98
This is the total amount of money you have paid toward interest	
Total Cost:	**$1,491.98**

What started as a $567.00 cost, buying now, pay later, costs almost $1500!

Use this to calculate the cost of using credit: https://www.practicalmoneyskills.com/resources/financial_calculators/credit_debt/credit_cost

https://www.wellsfargo.com/goals-credit/smarter-credit/manage-your-debt/total-cost-of-borrowing/

https://www.fool.com/the-ascent/credit-cards/articles/do-credit-cards-make-everything-more-expensive/

This credit trap started way back before the 1900s.

https://www.rockethq.com/learn/credit/the-history-of-credit

Basic Budgeting based on a paycheck.

What is a budget? It is a money plan. Want to know what successful people do to budget their paychecks?

Successful people save 10% to 20%, spend up to 75% on must-have, and spend 5%-10% on wants and "got to have its." Where people get in trouble is when they play roulette with the account. What this means is when you check your bank account balance and based on this amount, you spend it. But, lo and behold, you have automatic payments deducted to cover the insurance premium, car loan payment, rent, utilities, and other fixed payments. So, in essence, the bank balance may not be the actual bank balance! You have to list all the payments in the month, and the dates they are due to make sure you are always operating with the true bank balance.

For example, the bank balance shows an amount: $1330. You are happy when you see this and think you can have up to $1330 to spend (between pay periods). When this is the reality: (this is due between pay periods)

Item paid	Amount due
Car loan	$446.00
Car insurance	$270.00
Total	$716.00
Actual bank balance	$614.00

Where people get in trouble and have overdrafts is not taking into account the amount of money that gets taken out of the account for fixed expenses.

Now, let's continue.

The $614.00 is not the actual balance.

In this scenario, there is the electric bill to pay too. Not to forget the groceries and gas that have to be purchased. So, this $614.00 looks something like this:

Item paid	Amount due
Groceries (for 2 weeks)	$298.00
Gas for 2 weeks ($3.14 per gallon for 10-gallon tank, gassing once per week)	$62.28
Total ($614.00 minus $360.28)	$253.72 (left to save 10% and spend 20%)

Notice that in this case, there is $253.72 in discretionary funds (not spoken for with other bills and expenses). However, if there are credit card payments, student loan payments, and payments to family for debt rescue, that is all still deducted, and the discretionary funds are gone. When that happens, people reach for the plastic in their pocket, and well … you know what that's all about since it was covered already in this module.

Knowing what you know about credit and keeping watch over your bank account, Adulting gets easier without all the pitfalls that occur when you turn a blind eye to credit and bank accounts.

Want to know what the amount of your discretionary funds are? Go to our online course and complete the exercise. This is part of an online course Module 15 Keeping Track of Your Money exercise.

Health care/Self-care

Stress has become a part of life and is as inevitable as death and taxes. But, you do not have to let it run you down. This is where health care and self-care come into the picture. Making sure that you perform your job at your optimum is why so many Fortune 500 companies were having their employees take naps in nap pods while at the office (https://www.theguardian.com/business-to-business/2017/dec/04/clocking-off-the-companies-introducing-nap-time-to-the-workplace). Employers recognize the health benefit of their employees and the stress relief too. After waking from a nap, the person is refreshed and not stressed.

Now, it may not be that your employer has a nap pod, but you can have the same benefit by taking 5 minutes to breathe and relax. As we inhale and exhale, we are allowing our body to recharge in a similar way that a nap does. Our nervous system and endocrine system calms and our brain gets to rest. You can do this intentionally on a lunch break or during a 15-minute break. You just must want to treat yourself to a breathing break.

Health care and self-care go together when taking care of yourself.

Moving up the ladder of success often brings with it more responsibility and stress. Get in the habit of taking action to take care of yourself while you are in the process of climbing the ladder of success. This enhances your ability to be prepared, calm, relaxed, and restful.

Time Management To Live Your Life Stress-Free

The best way to live life with the greatest of ease and enjoyment is with a balanced life of work, family/friends, further personal and professional development, and fun. What this means is when juggling the obligations of work, family/friends, and school (for your career development), there needs to be a schedule that is intentional and disciplined. If any part of your life is out of balance, there are consequences resulting in added stress.

Here is an example of a weekly schedule that includes time for three aspects of life:

To DO items for the week of July 24-July 31	Home	Work	Business
The task	Paint the fence	Complete the software coding for new app (due July 28)	Do market research
Time doing this	After dinner Tuesday, July 26	Working 9 am - 2 pm Monday July 25 and completing project Wednesday July 27)	After 2 pm Monday, Tuesday, and Wednesday
The task	Mend the porch screen	Review co-worker software project (on July 28)	Get EIN
Time doing this	Sunday, July 24	After completing my project - will review co-worker project	While taking a lunch break Monday, July 25
The task	Date night		Complete and file Articles of Incorporation (self imposed deadline July 30
Time doing this	Friday night, July 29		July 29 during lunch break

Now that the list of items of what needs to get accomplished to cover all bases is made and determined which days and when in the day to do them, let's make a list of them per day of the week:

Days of the week	Tasks to accomplish		
Sunday, July 24	Mend the porch screen		
Monday, July 25	Work on a software project and complete by Wednesday, July 27	Get EIN	Do mark research
Tuesday, July 26	Paint the fence after dinner		Do mark research
Wednesday, July 27	Review tasks Mon-Wed and do what is not yet done		Do mark research
Thursday, July 28	Review co-worker project		
Friday, July 29	Date night!		
Saturday, July 30	Make sure the Articles of Incorporation are filed		
Sunday, July 31	Relax!		

This may seem over the top, but taking a bit of time to figure out a schedule such as this allows for a balanced life.

Life balance/Wheel of life

The Wheel of Life is an assessment tool you can use to uncover where there might be a balance issue in any or all of these aspects of your life:

Business and Career

Finances

Health

Family and friends

Romance

Personal development

Fun and recreation

Contribution/Giving Back

Go to our online course and take the Wheel of Life assessment as designed by **Paul J. Meyer**, founder of Success Motivation® Institute Inc. This is part of an online course Module 15 Wheel of Life exercise.

Finding a House/Apartment

Finding a place where you call home is challenging and takes effort in most cases. Then there are those cases where a friend invites you to be their roommate and the search for your place to call home is done.

When you are not invited to be a roommate and you are on your own to find a place to live. There are some tips to make the search easier and more enjoyable.

Make sure you know what you can afford to pay for a mortgage or rent. For example, the general rule is 30% of your take-home pay is allotted for housing. So, if your take-home pay for the month is

$2330, $699 is the highest you can go towards covering the rent or a mortgage.

Looking for rent in the $600 range is challenging since most places charge between $900 and $1200 for a one-bedroom apartment in a less populated area, and double to trip that in a more metropolitan area. If you agree to renting an apartment for $900 when your take-home monthly pay is $2330, you will have to maintain a tight budget to make sure that all your expenses do not go over $2330 — or find someone to invite you (or you invite them) to be your roommate and split the rent.

How to Do Taxes

are options for doing taxes.

You can have someone do them for you, or you can do them yourself.

You will pay a flat fee in the range of $50 - $900 depending on the tax situation. There are many tax preparers for you to choose from.

Nerdwallet has some good advice (click on the link)

(https://www.nerdwallet.com/article/taxes/how-to-find-best-tax-preparer-near)

1. Ask for a preparer tax identification number (PTIN)

The IRS requires anyone who prepares or assists in preparing federal tax returns for compensation to have a preparer tax identification number or PTIN. Note the phrase "for compensation" — volunteer tax preparers don't need PTINs. Make sure your income tax preparer puts their PTIN number on your return; the IRS requires that, too.

2. Require a CPA, law license, or enrolled agent designation

A PTIN is a basic requirement that's relatively easy to get, so it doesn't hurt to go a step further and seek out a credentialed preparer — someone who's also a certified public accountant

(CPA), licensed attorney, or enrolled agent (EA). The amount of ongoing study for each designation will vary, but these professionals are generally held to a higher standard of education and expertise.

You can also consider working with a tax pro who has completed the IRS' Annual Filing Season program. The Accredited Business Accountant/Advisor and Accredited Tax Preparer are examples of programs that help preparers fulfill the Annual Filing Season Program requirement.

How do you find the best tax preparer near you with the credentials you want? One way is to search the IRS's directory. It includes preparers with PTINs and IRS-recognized professional credentials. Volunteer preparers and preparers with just PTINs won't be in the database.

3. Look for friends in high places

Membership in a professional organization such as the National Association of Tax Professionals, the National Association of Enrolled Agents, the American Institute of Certified Public Accountants, or the American Academy of Attorney CPAs is always a good thing to have in a tax advisor, as most have codes of ethics, professional conduct requirements, and various certification programs.

If you already work with a financial advisor, check to see if they offer tax planning or advisory services. Their firm may be able to easily connect you with a tax advisor.

» Looking for more help? Compare the best wealth advisors.

4. Compare tax advisor fees

How much do tax preparers charge? According to a 2022 Drake Software survey of over 3,600 tax preparers in the United States, the average fee for preparing a non-itemized Form 1040 in 2023 is estimated to hover around $210. For an itemized Form 1040, that fee jumps to $256.

Often, tax preparers either charge a minimum fee, plus cost based on the complexity of your return, or they charge a set fee for each form and schedule needed in your return. If you come across a tax preparer whose fee is based on the size of your refund or who says they can get you a bigger refund than the next person, that's a red flag.

5. Reconsider tax advisors who don't e-file

The IRS requires any paid preparer who does more than 11 returns for clients to file electronically via the IRS's e-file system. If your tax preparer doesn't offer e-file capability, it may be a sign the person isn't doing as much tax prep as you thought.

6. Confirm they'll sign on the dotted line

The law requires paid preparers to sign their clients' returns and provide their PTINs. Never sign a blank tax return — the preparer could put anything on the return, including their bank account number so they can steal your refund.

7. Check if your advisor would have your back

Enrolled agents, CPAs, and attorneys with PTINs can represent you in front of the IRS on audits, payments and collection issues, and appeals. Preparers who just have PTINs can't — even if they prepared your return. Preparers who complete the Annual Filing Season Program can represent clients only in limited circumstances.

Availability is also crucial. Even after the filing season is over and your tax return is history, the best tax preparers will take your call, respond to your email, or welcome you for a visit.

If meeting with an advisor in person isn't critical, you may consider getting help online. Many online tax preparers now offer live assistance, so if you do have a question while you're filing, you can get help in real-time.

If you want to do your own taxes, there are several online tax software options.

Learn more from NerdWallet (https://www.nerdwallet.com/article/taxes/irs-free-file-tax-preparation-help)

Here are five ways to file your taxes for free.

1. IRS Free File

What it is

IRS Free File is a partnership between the IRS and a nonprofit organization called the Free File Alliance. IRS Free File provides access to free guided tax preparation software from several tax-prep companies, including major brands such as TaxAct and TaxSlayer. Some Free File products are also available in Spanish. Taxpayers can begin accessing Free File options via the IRS website on January 13.

Who is eligible?

Generally, you must fall beneath a certain income level to qualify, and the IRS estimates that 70% of all taxpayers are eligible. To qualify for IRS Free File in 2023, taxpayers must have had an adjusted gross income of $73,000 or less in 2022.

If your income is over the limit, IRS Free File also provides everyone with access to free fillable IRS forms that you can submit electronically at no additional cost. This option does not provide much tax guidance.

How it works

For best results, the IRS urges taxpayers to use their Free File Online Lookup Tool to get matched with a provider. The tool will run you through some basic questions about your filing status, age, home address, income and eligibility for certain credits. You can also manually browse through all the Free File offers.

Keep in mind that not all Free File offers include free state returns, so make sure to read through the fine print. However, according to the IRS, several states also have state Free File programs patterned after the federal one. That means you might be able to get free tax preparation for your state return, too.

Where to get Free File

IRS.gov/freefile or via the IRS2Go app. Even though some providers may advertise themselves as Free File participants on their website, the only way to ensure you're accessing a Free File offer is to go directly through the IRS first.

2. Direct-from-provider free tax preparation software

Many major tax software providers offer free tax preparation software for people with really simple tax situations. These packages may be different from what's available via IRS Free File.

Who is eligible?

How each provider defines "simple tax return" will vary. Typically (but not always), these packages work for people who only have income from one job and aren't itemizing on their tax returns.

How it works

- Most free packages cover Form 1040 and may help you to claim credits such as the child tax credit or the earned income tax credit.

- State tax returns are usually also included in these free packages, though some software providers tend to add a fee for that as the tax-filing deadline nears.

Our tax software roundup compares free online tax software from some of the biggest providers such as TurboTax and H&R Block.

3. Volunteer Income Tax Assistance (VITA)

A federal grant program that helps community organizations provide free tax preparation to low- and moderate-income individuals, the disabled, the elderly, and limited-English speakers.

Who is eligible

Generally, the income limit to qualify for free tax help is $60,000.

How it works

Free tax preparation from local, IRS-certified volunteers.

This might not work for you if your tax situation is complicated. For example, volunteers won't prepare Schedule C with losses (sorry, freelancers), complicated Schedule Ds (sorry, investors), or forms associated with nondeductible IRA contributions or determinations of worker status (i.e., whether you're technically an employee or an independent contractor).

The IRS website lists VITA sites across the country.

4. Tax Counseling for the Elderly (TCE)

A federal grant program that helps community organizations provide free tax preparation to low- and moderate-income individuals, the disabled, the elderly, and limited-English speakers.

What it is

A federal grant program that helps community organizations provide free tax preparation with a focus on pension and retirement-related tax issues.

Who is eligible?

Although the program was established to give free tax help to people 60 and older and still prioritizes that demographic, there is no minimum age requirement. Trained volunteers do the tax preparation.

How it works

Similar to VITA, community organizations, and nonprofits use grant money to provide free tax preparation. Most TCE sites are operated by the AARP Foundation's Tax-Aide program.

Where to get it

The IRS website lists TCE sites.

5. MilTax

What it is.

A Department of Defense program that provides free tax software from H&R Block, as well as financial and legal resources and other help to military members and their families.

How it works

In addition to free tax software, trained MilTax consultants can give free tax help by phone and via live chat. MilTax participates in the

VITA program, which means you also can get face-to-face free tax help on base or nearby.

Where to get it

Head to Militaryonesource.mil to get the software, find helpline numbers, and hours of operation and see if a nearby installation has a VITA site.

Grocery Shopping

Budgeting and going grocery shopping is sometimes a nightmare given the rise in pricing. This is where shopping with coupons and AI Apps https://budgetingforbliss.com/4-best-grocery-shopping-apps-to-save-money/

Adulting includes the discipline to buy food items that are nutritious and healthy. Shopping for food and other items on a budget can be tough and very challenging especially with rising costs taking place. So, it is recommended you might try doing these things.

https://health.clevelandclinic.org/10-expert-tips-grocery-shopping-budget/

Preventive cardiology dietitian Kate Patton, MEd, RD, CSSD, LD, shares 10 tips for smart shopping — and how to avoid draining your wallet.

1. Shop for nonperishable items online

Products like protein bars and dried fruits are ideal for buying from online retailers like Amazon or your local store's online site. It saves you money because you won't have to pay food tax and if shipping is free, that's an added incentive. Just be sure to check expiration dates.

2. Buy perishable foods in quantities you'll use

Spoiled food that's tossed into the garbage is no bargain. Try to buy fresh produce in small portions that you know you will eat within a week. For example, it's OK to split up bananas or grapes according to how many you need. Instead of buying mostly fresh produce, look for frozen fruits and vegetables, which are less perishable. and allow for portion-controlled servings. It also makes for healthy snacks and meals easily accessible, so you won't have an excuse not to load up on your fruits and veggies.

3. Buy fresh fruits and vegetables in season

You'll not only save cash, but you'll also enjoy the most wholesome food on the market. Print out a helpful list of produce and stick it on your fridge. This way, you'll always be aware of what's in season when you head to the grocery store.

Who doesn't love supporting their local businesses? Buying locally grown produce helps stimulate your local economy and you can also freeze it into smaller portion sizes.

4. Buy meat and cereals in bulk

"Each stroke of the knife in processing costs more at checkout," says Patton. "Buy in bulk and do it yourself to cut the costs."

Make it a goal to buy your meat and cereal in bulk. Patton recommends buying fresh pork loin and slicing it into low-fat loin chops at home, buying a roast and cubing it into chunks, or buying a chicken and cutting it up at home. If you're not a meat eater, consider beans as a low-cost protein source. Buy oatmeal in bulk instead of individual flavored packs that have added sugar and salt. Plus, they cost more.

5. Be an informed shopper

Keep your budget from inflating by sticking to your grocery list. Use those weekly mailers to plan out your grocery purchases for the week and take some time to compare prices for your favorite food from different stores. This helps prevent impulse buying, which can lead to the quick demise of your food budget.

"Forgo 'buy one, get one free' offers, too," says Patton. "Either you'll wind up buying foods you won't eat, or you'll pay an inflated price for the 'buy' item to cover the cost of the free one."

6. Limit your purchase of ready-prepared foods

Convenience is great until you have to pay more for it. Go to the deli or refrigerated sections for ready-made foods only on occasions when you're willing to pay more for the convenience. You pay a higher price to have someone else prepare the meal, and when you start keeping that in mind while you're shopping, you'll start to back away from the prepared food aisle.

7. Clip coupons with caution

Clipping and using coupons can feel like an accomplishment, but on the flip side, coupons may persuade you to purchase items you generally wouldn't buy.

"If the coupon is for an item you can use, look for stores that give double coupon redemption for extra savings," she says.

8. Use your imagination with leftovers

The possibilities are endless when it comes to using your creativity to work with leftovers. Create soups, casseroles, and new dishes with your leftovers to avoid tossing out unused food. If you run short of ideas, browse websites for recipes and just key in your leftover ingredients.

9. Look for outlet stores such as day-old bakeries

Buying products from these outlet stores can help you stick to your grocery budget.

"Prices are reduced by more than 50% from store prices," says Patton. "Bread products freeze well and are versatile. You can use them in sandwiches, in recipes calling for breadcrumbs and stuffing."

10. Avoid portion-controlled snack packs

Not only are they more costly, they may not save you calories, either.

"Remember that fat-free doesn't mean sugar-free, and vice versa," she warns. "Always keep an eye out for the labels to decide if these snack packs are worth the splurge."

Insurance

Insurance for car, life, home, health, dental, short-term and long-term disability, catastrophic health, renters, boats and RVs, pets, travel, business,…

You may ask, why have insurance?

Auto insurance is mandatory by law.

Life insurance takes care of your loved ones after you are gone as they are taking care of the disposition of your body and debts.

Home insurance takes care of you when something happens (such as a flood, fire, or tornado) when you are looking to repair or rebuild after the disaster occurred. Most banks and mortgage companies make this mandatory and a condition of receiving the loan.

Health insurance takes care of you for regular check-ups and the times when you are injured or sick and need specialized care. Without this insurance, there is a lot of money owed to clinics, labs, hospitals, and pharmacies to cover the expenses for diagnosis, treatment, and medicine.

Dental insurance is often separate insurance from health insurance and it is highly recommended you get this too. You never know when you get a toothache that won't quit and must be attended to and treated. And — to make sure that never happens, you need to see a dentist twice a year for cleanings and check-ups, (and of course, always brush your teeth and floss between the teeth) — it is no fun to have to deal with a cavity in between the teeth!

Short-term and long-term disability is usually covered by your employer, but you might need to contribute to it too. Why get this? Well, it is not a good day when you are laid up due to an injury, can't work, and you are not getting a paycheck. This type of insurance at least gives you some portion of your regular pay during the period you can't work.

Catastrophic care insurance is for those times when you hear the word "cancer" or something else that is life-threatening. There is usually a long period of doctor visits, lab appointments, treatment center appointments, and maybe even physical therapy appointments and this takes you off work and out of commission for some time. The costs incurred for health care at a time when you still need to cover the bills can be way overwhelming. This type of insurance pays you to cover these costs as you recover.

Renter's insurance is sometimes required by the Landlord and covers your belongings in the case of fire, flood, or building damage should they be damaged.

Boats, RV, Off-road vehicle, and motorcycle coverage takes care of times when something unexpected and damaging occurs. In times like that, you may need to repair or replace your item and it gets costly. You get some money from the insurance company to cover the costs.

Pet insurance is always nice to have especially if you have a dog or cat. Have you been to a veterinarian clinic lately with your dog or cat? The cost of taking care of a bowser or kitty is very costly!

Travel insurance is especially nice to have in cases when your luggage ends up in the black hole, you become ill and either cancel or cut short your trip, or something happens weather-wise or with the carrier that prevents you from taking the trip. Whatever you paid for the trip is reimbursed per the terms of the insurance policy (read that by the way).

There are different types of business insurance coverage: General Liability, Commercial Property, Commercial Auto, Workman's Comp, Business Income, Board of Directors, Errors & Omissions, Data Breach, and Umbrella.

You must pay your monthly premium so that your insurance policy does not lapse and become invalid. At times, when things go as unplanned and unexpected, and there are damages, you'll be glad you have a valid and active insurance policy!

Retirement - NEVER too early...Stats

~~People are living longer and need to have a source of income that sustains them after retirement.~~
https://www.everydayhealth.com/senior-health/what-life-expectancy-today/

To get an idea of how much money you need in your retirement, use this calculator.

https://www.calculator.net/retirement-calculator.html

Now go to our online training course and learn how to save the money needed for when you retire. This is part of an online course Module 15 Saving money for retirement assignment.

Pay Yourself First!

This is a rule to live by. Make sure that when you get your take-home pay, you are spending it according to a carefully created budget that includes savings. Then take that percentage of the pay and put it in the savings/investment accounts. Ten percent is a reasonable rule of thumb for your set aside. That way you are not tempted to cheat yourself out of the money you need when you retire and need that money to live.

Simple Car Maintenance

Breaking down on the side of the road ruins the day/night, is costly, and time-consuming. So, taking your car to get the oil changed, tires rotated, and intermittent system checks ensures your vehicle takes you where you want to go without incident.

Basic House Maintenance and Handling Emergencies

Here is a list of items to do before moving in:
https://homebuyer.com/wp-content/uploads/2022/06/Homebuyer_HomeMaintenance_Printables.pdf

After living in the home, there are regular maintenance tasks to do to ensure your home is safe to live in Here is a list provided by the folks at American Family Insurance. They have several different lists of tasks done monthly, biannually, annually, seasonally, and year-round.

Check it out:

https://www.amfam.com/resources/articles/at-home/home-maintenance-checklist

Entrepreneurship & Gig Economy

Back to the scenario of earning $2330 per month and having to find a place to live. If no one invites you to be their roommate, or you could not get anyone to accept your invitation, then you will need to find and fund the apartment rent on your own. If you want to work with a bigger, better budget and not a tight knit one, you will need to have to make more income to subsidize what you make at your full-time job. This means having a side gig/side hustle.

More and more people are getting involved in having a side business in some form. They are either bootstrapping the start of a business out of their home or getting involved in a side hustle with a company such as Uber, Lyft, Postmates, Uber Eats, Amazon, etc.

For help locating a side gig-side hustle, go to https://gigworker.com/ or https://www.entrepreneur.com/growing-a-business/18-freelance-sites-to-find-your-next-gig/349238. This is a great way to locate a flexible part-time gig with a company that would hire you as a freelancer.

If you want to be your own boss and eventually fire your boss, then you will need to know what steps to take to build, operate, sustain, and scale your own business.

Go to the online training course and get the training to be a successful entrepreneur. This is part of an online course Module 15 Entrepreneurship exercise.

Giving Back — Give Before You Get

"It is more blessed to give, than to receive." Act 20:35

Knowing that you somehow lifted the burden of a fellow human being with your donation of time, talent, or treasure warms your heart and makes you feel good. But it does more than that; you become more valued and valuable to this world. Giving yourself freely to help another person out is the greatest feeling ever. Knowing that you are making a difference in someone's life gives greater meaning to your life. Not only that but the universe has a way of returning kindness to you from giving kindness to others.

Etiquette — Working from Home and Working in the Office

What a privilege it is to work at home! For many people, working at home is the "utopia" of work! In a work-at-home work environment, you get to balance home and work. Instead of fitting life into work you, get to fit work into life since you are working autonomously and without the physical presence of your boss. But that does not mean the "when the cat's away, the mice shall play" scenario. No, what this means is you are trusted with the responsibilities given to you and expected to come through with all the tasks it takes to get the job done. This may include attending meetings virtually and being prepared to do your part. This may also mean that you will have deliverables with deadlines and must do what is needed to submit quality work on time. Failing to comply with what is expected could likely terminate the work-at-home work arrangement. So, it is beneficial to you to heed this guidance.

Do

Show up to your virtual work on time (or even 10 - 15 minutes early) for your shift.

Be prepared to contribute to the work conversation at the virtual team meetings.

Be dressed appropriately (don't be wearing pajamas top)

Be groomed appropriately (don't look like you just rolled out of bed) even though that may be the case.

Comb your hair and look freshened and energized.

Don't

Be late to the meeting.

Fail to show up for work.

Submit work late.

Submit low-quality work.

Following these guidelines will ensure your work-at-home experience goes well and continues without end.

Ethical Behavior/Decision Making

When it comes to ethical behavior and ethical decision-making, it is no joke and must be taken seriously. Failing to act ethically or making an unethical decision could result in dire consequences. You could ruin your career or even others' careers just by your action or inaction.

Most people behave unethically when they feel like their back is against the wall or they are boxed in and have no way out. In a moment such as that, the best thing to do is take a breath and give yourself a moment to not do anything. Dan Low, a world-renowned corporate trainer and a master of mind mending teaches us to turn our head to the right. When you turn your head to the right, your brain takes a momentary recess and allows the emotion of fear and anger to instantly leave so that you have a clear mind to decide your next move.

Having the clear mind to decide to go right or go left or stay still is what will save you from making the unethical decision to behave unethically.

So, the next time you feel like you are boxed in, and your back is against the wall, take a breath and turn your head to the right. You'll truly be amazed at how that helps!

It's not all black and white —- it depends.

So, back to having made a decision.

Sometimes we just want to know that what we are dealing with can be reasoned with a point-blank or black-and-white reason.

Example: graduating high school and asking, "should I go to college or get a full-time job?" Answer: It depends.

Example: got notified my job position is changing and my department is dissolving. Should I look for another type of job with the same company? Should I look for another company with an open job position that matches my current skills? Should I retrain to reskill? Answer to all these questions: It depends.

In my mid-thirties being bombarded with ads, text messages, and phone calls to invest a portion of my paycheck. Should I engage in investing or not? Answer: It depends.

Do I do this, or do I do that questions in life cannot be readily answered, even though we wish they could be. It is a bit uncomfortable to be dangling with a decision, and we want instant answers. But in the case of all three scenarios, it depends on several factors.

It depends on

Your goals and timeline are attached to them.

Your skills and abilities and interests.

Whether or not you need or want instant gratification.

Whether or not you can live with a certain level of risk.

Are you beginning to understand why the answer is "It depends?"

Making life-impacting decisions takes time, effort, energy, and research to determine the best course of action that meets your goals.

Diversity, Equity, Inclusion, and Belonging

DEI&B are more than buzzwords, they have become embedded in legal statutes.

What exactly does this mean? This means the attention and focus are on treating everyone with dignity and value.

Diversity simply refers to the society and community of people from different backgrounds, races, religions, sexual orientations, or any other factor that places them in a categorical segment of the population. In times past, these categorical segments of the population received treatment that was different from other segments of the population. But recently, all people of the population have begun to experience fair, and equitable treatment and consideration.

So, what does equity mean?

Well, **equity** does not mean the same as equality. Consider this picture.

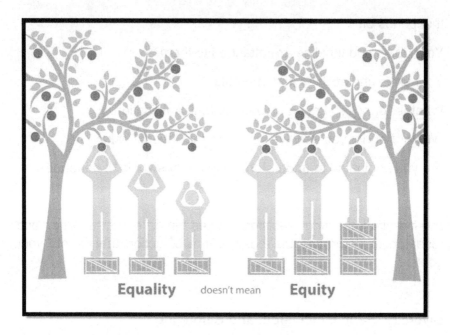

(Photo by Google Images- public domain)

You will notice that on the **equality** side, all three people are standing on crates, but only one is reaching the fruit. On the other side, where equity is in play, all three people are reaching the fruit standing on the appropriate number of crates needed to reach the fruit. In an equitable situation, everyone gets what they need to succeed.

Side note: College is the great equalizer! All college people are treated equitably and are provided with an education by which they develop skills, knowledge, and abilities needed for gainful employment. This means no matter what may have occurred in the past, in the present, building a future to accomplish lifetime goals is possible. The building of a future that is bright and full of promise includes anyone and everyone!

>>> (Optional) **This is why we advocate that having an e-portfolio highlights accomplishments and demonstrates skills**

for everyone that partakes in the exercise of creating an e-portfolio<<<.

Inclusion refers to the acknowledgment and acceptance of others. No one is left out or left behind. All are invited to participate. In times past, this was not the case. What happened to some segments of the population made it so they were uninvited and left out of what other segments of the population were allowed to do and participate in. Not anymore. All people are invited and encouraged to fully partake and participate in all that life has to offer.

So, how is inclusion any different than belonging (you might ask)?

Belonging is a sense, whereas inclusion is a privilege. When you feel like you belong at some place or in something, you feel at home and at ease. This is what everyone is encouraged to make possible so that everyone feels welcomed, appreciated, and valued.

Brainstorming Techniques

When there is a decision to be made, it is best to think of all possible options. When you brainstorm, all thoughts or options are welcome. This is not the time to be critical of any option that pops into your mind, or in the minds of others should your brainstorming session be in a group.

Here are some techniques to consider when having a brainstorming session:https://www.proofhub.com/articles/brainstorming-techniques

Here are the five brainstorming techniques that help you deliver excellence.

1. Associative Brainstorming

This exercise can be done solo or by several people where they sit down at a quiet place with a pen and paper. Now, you just need an idea, probably a single word that summarizes the idea in a nutshell. Start writing other words that come up in your mind associated with that idea or a word. It works best when you let your mind run free and try to come up with as many words as possible. With this technique, you tend to trigger your mind with other related words that further trigger new words. This allows your brain to connect the dots and conceive several new ideas. You can easily choose the duration of exercise, anything from 10 minutes to an hour.

2. Brainwriting

This is a group exercise where some team members sit down to work on an idea. This is polymorphic i.e., the idea can take different forms as it progresses. In this activity, a team leader shares the topic, and the team members are required to write three ideas on a piece of paper and pass it to the other members. Now, likewise, they will jot down three ideas in coherence with the previous ideas and pass them on. Similarly, this will be repeated until the last person is done with their input.

After the activity is performed, sit down and go through all the ideas. You will likely need to scrap some of them. Some might trigger better ideas as well. With a little more brainstorming, you can transform the average ideas into incredible ones.

3. Freestorming

Free Storming is usually thinking and writing about anything and everything that comes to your mind whenever you think of an idea. You just need to find a quiet place and allow yourself to completely immerse yourself in free storming. Just note down all the things – relevant or irrelevant, good or bad in your notebook or a computer. This is a powerful brainstorming technique that lets you put down all the 'real and raw' ideas and then take a deep dive into an ocean of possibilities where many hidden ideas are waiting to be discovered.

4. Virtual Brainstorming

Virtual brainstorming is often referred to as online brainstorming and is known as one of the best brainstorming techniques. Today, when most of the teams are geographically scattered, more and more people are opting for this contemporary way of brainstorming. All you need is an internet connection, and you are all set to brainstorm!

5. *Rolestorming*

This probably is one of the most fun and engaging ways of brainstorming developed recently. Here, you don't think like yourself, rather you try to put yourself in someone else's shoes. Interestingly, it allows you to think about how you would think if you were somebody else. Your boss? Or maybe your mentor?

You can give it a spin-off by thinking like Warren Buffett, Steve Jobs, or maybe Barack Obama. Now, with this activity, you can shed all your inhibitions and limitations aside and allow yourself to think like stalwarts. They say, "Fake it till you make it". This is a great way to develop new ideas without losing your authenticity and at the same time stepping into the world of the Greats.

Engaging in LIFE

Not sitting on the bleachers and watching others on the field is engaging in life.

Playing on the field of what's possible as a player makes life new and exciting! Being prepared to do your part in the game is what makes it possible to score and win in life.

No matter the challenge, having the right skills, the right tools, and the right strategy for your life is what helps you move forward.

Having the compass that is right for you to reach your NorthStar is your game plan. That's what this course is all about; it gives you what you need to have your compass leading you to your NorthStar, your lifetime dream.

It is possible to have what you want, live every day with joy, and can't wait to get to your job where you do what you love and love what you do.

We invite you to stay in touch with Future Forward Academy and be a lifetime learner.

Chapter Summary

- Living life and overcoming challenges takes skills, determination, discipline, and knowledge.

- Having the willpower to put into action what you learn from this chapter and more information to come on the website Futureforwardacademy.com will serve you well for having a stress-free and more blissful life while adulting.

The Question:

How do I best manage my personal finances and plan for long-term success?

The AI Response:

1. Create a budget: A budget is a key tool for managing your personal finances and planning for long-term success. It will help you track your spending and keep you on track.

2. Set financial goals: Having financial goals will help you stay focused and motivated. Think about short-term and long-term goals, such as saving for retirement, buying a house, or paying down debt.

3. Save for the future: One of the most important things you can do for your financial future is to save regularly. Set up an automatic transfer from your checking to your savings account each month and make sure you're contributing to a retirement account.

4. Pay off debt: Paying off debt can be one of the best ways to improve your financial standing. Prioritize paying off high-interest debt first, such as credit cards and student loans.

5. Invest wisely: Investing can be a great way to grow your money over time. Research different investing options and do your best to diversify your portfolio.

6. Live within your means: It's important to remember that you can't buy everything you want. Spend only what you can afford and don't rely on credit cards to cover expenses.

Author's Comment on AI Response:

The number one "rule" I might add is "Pay Yourself First". I often recommend taking 10% off the top, in addition to maxing out 401K contributions if available, especially if they are matched by your employer. You also want to set aside a portion for charitable contributions. Stick to your budget as mentioned above. You might want to create a Fidelity, E*TRADE, or Robin Hood account and experiment with it to get some investing experience. The overriding recommendation to keep in mind is to spend less than you make and pay off credit cards EVERY month.

16 ETHICAL CONSIDERATIONS & LIFETIME SUCCESS

You are who you say and what you do.

"Do not judge me by my successes. Judge me by how many times I fell down and got back up again.

Nelson Mandela

What this chapter covers:

- You will be challenged
- Options to react
- Let's practice and be ready!

When you break down the word **ETHICS**, you get this:

Embrace

Truth

Help

Individuals

Create

Success

Thinking and acting in this manner leaves very little wiggle room for acting selfishly. For society to benefit from ethical thoughts and actions, the approach to take is to consider actions with honor, intelligence, and much consideration. This will oftentimes mean taking the high road and not the easy way out. Ultimately, you might be making a difficult decision that may not be popular, but instead will be the most beneficial to society and your long-term well-being.

Embracing truth simply means that you are open and honest in your thoughts and actions. Acting honorably and not deceitfully is what needs to be considered ethical. When faced with a situation that you feel is not right, having the courage to deal with it ethically often comes from knowing and caring how what you do will affect others. It may surprise you, but the decision you make at that moment does not only affect you, but others may have to live with the consequences of your decision.

Look at this chart and see a listing of moments when unethical behavior occurred and what may remedy the situation. Retrieved from Five Barriers to an ethical organization | Good work ethic, Ethics, Essay (pinterest.com)

ILL-CONCEIVED GOALS	MOTIVATED BLINDNESS	INDIRECT BLINDNESS	THE SLIPPERY SLOPE	OVERVALUING OUTCOMES
DESCRIPTION We set goals and incentives to promote a desired behavior, but they encourage a negative one.	We overlook the unethical behavior of others when it's in our interest to remain ignorant.	We hold others less accountable for unethical behavior when it's carried out through third parties.	We are less able to see others' unethical behavior when it develops gradually.	We give a pass to unethical behavior if the outcome is good.
EXAMPLE The pressure to maximize billable hours in accounting, consulting, and law firms leads to unconscious padding.	Baseball officials failed to notice they'd created conditions that encouraged steroid use.	A drug company deflects attention from a price increase by selling rights to another company, which imposes the increase.	Auditors may be more likely to accept a client firm's questionable financial statements if infractions have accrued over time.	A researcher whose fraudulent clinical trial saves lives is considered more ethical than one whose fraudulent trial leads to deaths.
REMEDIES Brainstorm unintended consequences when devising goals and incentives. Consider alternative goals that may be more important to reward.	Root out conflicts of interest. Simply being aware of them doesn't necessarily reduce their negative effect on decision making.	When handing off or outsourcing work, ask whether the assignment might invite unethical behavior and take ownership of the implications.	Be alert for even trivial ethical infractions and address them immediately. Investigate whether a change in behavior has occurred.	Examine both "good" and "bad" decisions for their ethical implications. Reward solid decision processes, not just good outcomes.

Considering the benefit to the community and society over the benefit to self is the highest form of ethics and one we should all be doing.

Count On Being Challenged

Without a doubt, there is a moment coming when you will be faced with an ethical dilemma. The fact that we live in a time and place where the actions and behaviors of ourselves affect a great many people, means that we have to intentionally act with ETHICS. Retrieved from PPT - Professional Ethics PowerPoint Presentation, free download - ID:2914760 (slideserve.com)

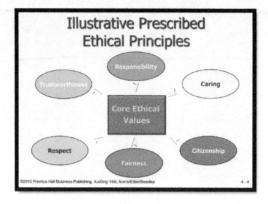

Let's take a quick look at the principles in the total illustrative prescribed ethical principles:

RESPONSIBILITY: owning your actions and not looking to blame anyone or anyone for what happened or did not happen in your life and work.

CARING: looking at someone's need and having the desire to help fulfill that need.

CITIZENSHIP: doing your part so that others can live in peace, safety, and security, and may prosper

FAIRNESS: living your life with actions that are just and fair to all human beings

RESPECT: behaving toward others with regard to their uniqueness with acceptance and value

TRUSTWORTHINESS: walk the talk, talk the walk ---your actions align with what you say you will or will not do --- you can be trusted your word is your bond to your deeds

Core ethical values are inside all of us! We are born with them and along the way, we see them in others (or not). At any rate, as human beings, we have innate ethical qualities whether we know them or not, they are within us. As early as Kindergarten, these ethical qualities begin to surface. Have you ever had the moment to watch children between the ages of 4 years old and 6 years old play together? There are scenes of selfishness mixed with scenes of sharing. The scenes of sharing are mostly after there is prompting from the teacher to do so. However, some children will naturally see the needs of another child and meet that need. Such as in the story of student-to-student caring.

In the book, *"Pulling Each Other Along,"* there are several heartwarming stories of people caring for others, but the one really extraordinary story is about one student that took the time and trouble to help another student so that their fellow student did not miss out on a field trip. You see, one student was severely disabled and could not walk and was very afraid for the day the class was to take a field trip to the museum. Seeing that their fellow student was very afraid of the field trip, they brought with them to school a wagon so that their fellow student would ride in the wagon while the other people walked from the bus to the museum and all around the museum. This extraordinary measure made by one student on behalf of the other student happened to occur in elementary school.

For this story and others like it, get the book: Pulling Each Other Along, written by Todd Civin and Doug Cornfield,

We human beings operate best when we are not acting in fear, anger, or stress. More than likely, unethical behavior comes in those moments when someone feels pressured, and their backs are up against a wall. It is in those moments we need to find a way to take control of our emotions so that we can gain control of our environment and the situations we may be facing. It is possible to take control of our emotions, it just takes time and practice.

Options to React

There are always options with a course of action that may seem easy and tempting to take that could end up in disaster. It takes a person intentionally practicing ETHICS to choose the right path.

Let's practice

>>> (Optional) The online training course has practical exercises for you to gain and strengthen the skill of ETHICS. This is part of an online course Module 16 Ethics Exercise.

Chapter Summary

We have all been victims (indirect and indirect impact) of someone or some company not acting ethically. If you have not nodded your head with this statement, then think about the times someone (maybe even you) was scammed. Think of those times you were deceived, cheated, or lied to by a person or company you trusted. How about times when you know of someone or some company committing fraud? And how about identity theft or when the computer is struck with malicious software like ransomware?

When on the receiving end of unethical behavior, we do not feel safe and often feel betrayed. If we do not control our emotions and act impulsively, we may cause betrayal to someone close to us (direct impact), or to others relying on us to behave ethically (indirect impact) causing them harm. In the moment of behaving unethically, we have essentially unraveled our progress in life and career. This is what we intend to keep you from doing with this chapter and our future courses.

The Question:

What are the top considerations for living an ethical and honorable life?

The AI Response:

1. Respect for the rights and well-being of others.

2. Honesty and integrity in all interactions.

3. Responsibility for one's actions and decisions.

4. Respect for the environment and natural resources.

5. A commitment to justice and fairness.

6. A commitment to personal growth and self-improvement.

7. A commitment to truth and knowledge.

8. A commitment to service and community involvement.

9. A commitment to spiritual and moral development.

10. A commitment to human rights and the rule of law.

Author's Comment on AI Response:

You may have heard of the Golden Rule "Do unto others as you would have others do unto you". I prefer the Platinum Rule ``Do unto others as they would want to be done unto themselves". Trying to walk in someone else's shoes and understanding their needs is a powerful opportunity to foster empathy and develop an understanding of another person's needs and wants. Filling their needs, as opposed to yours, gives you powerful insights when working with others. Another ethical consideration to be aware of is that once trust is broken, it is very difficult to restore that trust. ALWAYS deal honestly and honorably. Your reputation travels with you everywhere throughout your life.

17 PARTNERING WITH ARTIFICIAL INTELLIGENCE (AI): CAREER IMPACT

"It's not AI that's going to take your job, but someone who knows how to use AI might."

Aaron Mok of *Business Insider*

What this chapter covers:

- Realism and reaction to Artificial Intelligence.

- Impact on future careers.

- Impact on ethics.

A lot of attention is being paid to Artificial Intelligence (AI). So how can it help land the opportunities that I seek? Let's take a closer look.

AI can take many forms. A variety of industries actively use it to make decisions. It is sometimes said that Amazon, Alphabet (Google), and Meta (Facebook) know more about us than we know about ourselves. When online, we are sent ads and articles that relate to other online activities we have participated in. Companies are pre-screening resumes using ATS (Applicant Tracking Systems) that work to determine the candidates that best fit the needs of the organization.

AI is generating art, stories, music, articles, press releases, advertising, and essay answers. Not too long ago, at a Pueblo, Colorado State Fair art contest, an AI-generated artwork won first place in the fine art competition. Though many of the artists participating objected to a non-human-created piece of art being awarded the first-place prize, as no rules were violated, and the art was generated by a human using text to describe the art that the AI was to create (used a tool called Midjourney), the artist was able to keep the prize and first-place blue ribbon. Pretty soon, if not already, your next favorite song and lyrics might be AI-generated!

First place fine arts contest winner 2022 Pueblo, Colorado State Fair

One particular tool that is easily accessed and holds amazing promise for NLP (Natural Language Processing) is an AI Chatbot called ChatGPT-3.5 released on 11/30/22 by OpenAI. An update, GPT-4, was released on 3/14/23. Head on over to https://beta.openai.com/playground and check it out (note: 3.5 is free while GPT-4 requires a monthly subscription fee). I might call this a "Google on steroids". You can have a "conversation" in plain English, and it responds quickly and with reasonable accuracy, but be warned! The answers given are based on a fixed dataset from 2021 and prior. The data is not updated dynamically. There is a term called GIGO, typically translated as Garbage In Garbage Out. I have another translation, of Garbage in Gospel Out, as the results of ChatGPT queries are sometimes treated as gospel and considered accurate. The reality is you need to be careful as they are often inaccurate, slanted, or provide answers without depth.

So, if this tool is so flawed, why use it? The answer is that you can get some pretty good answers, and if not deep, the answers can be used as a springboard to generate more questions and answers. You can ask about resumes and content. You can inquire as to how to answer specific questions. You can use it as a company research tool. If you are aware of the potential limitations, you can take advantage of what this tool does have to offer.

The following is a sample dialog with ChatGPT. The questions were initiated by the author. The answers were directly generated by ChatGBT. The content and response posts can also be found in the LinkedIn newsletter, Career Capsule (where you can also subscribe), at https://www.linkedin.com/pulse/ai-interview-covering-career-topics-chatgbt-dr-scott/.

Q1: how do i prepare for a job interview

1. Research the company and the position: Before your interview, make sure you do your homework and research the company and the position you are interviewing for. This includes their mission and

values, products and services, recent news and events, their competitors, and anything else relevant to the role you are interviewing for.

2. Prepare answers to common interview questions: Most job interviews include some common questions. Take some time to practice your answers to these questions, such as "Tell me about yourself" and "What are your greatest strengths and weaknesses?"

3. Prepare questions for the interviewer: Come prepared with questions to ask the interviewer. This could include questions about the team, the company's culture, and the day-to-day responsibilities of the role.

4. Dress appropriately: Make sure to dress professionally for the interview and look your best. This will show the interviewer that you take the opportunity seriously.

5. Arrive early: Make sure to arrive at least 10-15 minutes early for the interview. This will give you time to get settled and relaxed before the interview starts. 6. Follow up: After the interview, make sure to follow up with a thank you note and an email.

Q2: how do i figure out what i want for a career

1. Take an assessment: Taking an assessment can help you figure out what type of job might be a good fit for you. There are a variety of free online assessments that can help you narrow down your career options.

2. Research different careers: Take some time to research different career paths and industries that interest you. Read job descriptions and talk to people in the field to get a better understanding of the roles and responsibilities.

3. Identify your skills and qualities: Make a list of your skills, abilities, and qualities. This will help you identify which jobs or industries might be a good fit.

4. Narrow down your options: Once you have identified some potential career options, narrow down your list to a few that you are most interested in.

5. Plot out a plan: Once you have narrowed down your list, create a plan to pursue your desired career. This could include setting goals, taking classes, and networking with people in the field.

Q3: What are some good free career assessments

1. Myers-Briggs Type Indicator (MBTI) 2.

2. CareerExplorer

3. Skills Profiler by O*NET

4. Truity Personality Tests

5. Strong Interest Inventory

6. Career Values Card Sort

7. Job and Career Matchmaker

8. The Occupational Information Network (O*NET) Interest Profiler

9. The Holland Code

10. Career Path Self-Assessment

Q4: What are some URL links to the above assessments?

1.   Myers-Briggs   Type   Indicator   (MBTI):
https://www.16personalities.com/free-personality-test

2. CareerExplorer: https://www.careerexplorer.com/career-test/

3. Skills Profiler by O*NET: https://www.mynextmove.org/explore/ip

4. Truity Personality Tests: https://www.truity.com/test/type-finder-personality-test

5. Strong Interest Inventory: https://www.cpp.com/products/strong/

6. Career Values Card Sort: https://www.careerplanner.com/Career-Values-Card-Sort.cfm

7. Job and Career Matchmaker: https://www.onetonline.org/find/

8. The Occupational Information Network (O*NET) Interest Profiler: https://www.mynextmove.org/explore/ip

9. The Holland Code: https://www.careerkey.org/holland-codes/

10. Career Path Self-Assessment (Click on link)

https://www.livecareer.com/quintessential/

Q5: Write an article on choosing your career.

Choosing a career can be one of the most daunting decisions of your life. With so many options and potential paths, it can be difficult to know where to start. It's important to take the time to research and explore all of your options before committing to a career. Here are a few tips to help you find the right job for you.

First, assess your skills, interests, and values. Think about what you do best, what you enjoy doing, and what is important to you. This will help you narrow down your search and make it easier to find an occupation that you'll be passionate about.

Next, research the different types of jobs available. You can do this by talking to professionals in the field, looking at job postings, and reading industry publications. This will give you an idea of the types of skills and qualifications that employers are looking for.

Once you have an idea of the type of career you'd like to pursue, it's time to start networking. Connect with people in your chosen field and get their advice on what it takes to succeed. This will help you gain a better understanding of the industry and give you valuable insight into what it's really like to (note: purposely limited ChatGBT length of article. It cut off mid-sentence).

Q6: What are the best colleges for accounting?

1. University of Illinois at Urbana-Champaign

2. University of Pennsylvania

3. New York University

4. University of Texas at Austin

5. University of Southern California

6. Brigham Young University

7. University of Notre Dame

8. University of Michigan

9. University of Florida

10. University of California, Berkeley

Q7: What are the top 10 LinkedIn tips?

1. Complete Your Profile: A complete profile creates a strong impression and is more likely to be found by recruiters.

2. Get Endorsements: Once your profile is complete, ask for endorsements from colleagues, clients, and partners.

3. Join Groups: Join relevant groups related to your industry and start engaging in conversations.

4. Showcase Your Work: Post articles, videos, and presentations that showcase your work.

5. Ask For Recommendations: Ask former colleagues, bosses, and clients to write recommendations for you.

6. Connect With Employees: Connect with employees of companies you'd like to work for and follow their updates.

7. Research Companies: Use LinkedIn to research companies and understand their culture, products, and services.

8. Follow Influencers: Follow influencers and thought leaders in your field to stay up to date with industry news and trends.

9. Follow Companies: Follow companies you're interested in to stay informed about job openings and events.

10. Network: Use LinkedIn to network with professionals and build relationships.

Q8: Top 10 resume tips

1. Highlight Your Accomplishments: Make sure you are showcasing your biggest professional accomplishments that are most relevant to the job you are applying for.

2. Keep it Concise: Focus on quality rather than quantity. Make sure your resume is no more than two pages long – employers don't have time to read through a long, drawn out resume.

3. Tailor Your Resume to the Job: Before you even start writing your resume, make sure you research the job and tailor it to meet the job's requirements.

4. Use Action Words: Make sure to use powerful action words that convey your skills and accomplishments.

5. Make it Easily Readable: Use clear, concise language, and make sure to proofread your resume for any typos or errors.

6. Be Specific: Don't just list your job duties – describe how you achieved success and show the impact you had.

7. Showcase Your Technical Skills: Include any programming or software skills you may have in order to stand out.

8. List Your Education: Make sure to list your educational achievements, including any awards, honors, or certifications you may have.

Q9: Best books on choosing a career

1. What Color Is Your Parachute? 2020: A Practical Manual for Job-Hunters and Career-Changers by Richard N. Bolles

2. Designing Your Life: How to Build a Well-Lived, Joyful Life by Bill Burnett and Dave Evans

3. The Pathfinder: How to Choose or Change Your Career for a Lifetime of Satisfaction and Success by Nicholas Lore

4. Do What You Are: Discover the Perfect Career for You Through the Secrets of Personality Type by Paul D. Tieger and Barbara Barron-Tieger

5. StrengthsFinder 2.0 by Tom Rath

6. Finding Your Element: How to Discover Your Talents and Passions and Transform Your Life by Ken Robinson

7. The Defining Decade: Why Your Twenties Matter—And How to Make the Most of Them Now by Meg Jay

8. Reinventing You: Define Your Brand, Imagine Your Future by Dorie Clark

9. I Could Do Anything If I Only Knew What It Was: How to Discover What You Really Want and How to Get It by Barbara Sher

10. What's Next?: Finding Your Passion and Your

As you can see, this powerful tool generates some amazing conversational results. Although not impressed with the LinkedIn answers above, many of the other suggestions, including the reading list and assessment tool list/links, can help someone seeking career advice to a solid base from which to take action.

>>> (Optional) If you want to get started with practicing to use AI, go to the online module 17 exercise: Partnering with AI Workbook.

Other AI tools, such as https://app.grammarly.com/ and https://quillbot.com/, can help with editing cover letters, emails, resumes, and LinkedIn profiles. A nice overview of AI categories and apps can be found at (see picture)

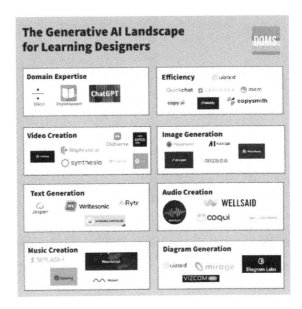

Happy Hunting!

EPILOG

Wherever your compass takes you down whatever path, you are on the right track for YOU.

You read this book, did the exercises, took the course, and are ready to move forward, taking steps to a lifetime of success, joy, and fulfillment.

Along the path, please keep in mind the following:

- Looking for a full-time job is a full-time job:

- Process overview

- Self-care ---

Self-care before, during, and after the search.

Breathe > take a breath > breathing clears the mind.

Move > Turn your head to the right when something happens, and you get upset.

Feel good about yourself > You are making progress. Just like taking one step after another, you are going from point A to point B on your way to point C.

Balance - even though this is a full-time job, take care of yourself.

Make time for yourself to relax. Scientists have shown that a clear mind comes from breathing and doing things we like. So, make time to do them!

Eat a proper diet. Too much snack food interrupts proper digestion, and since your immunity is in your gut, you must ensure it is healthy.

Get proper sleep. Scientists have also shown that the mind and body cannot function properly without proper rest. Adults need between 7-9 hours of sleep. Consider your physical, mental, and spiritual well-being.

Your physical stamina, believe it or not, helps with work stamina. If you are out of shape, you tend to get tired more easily and cannot take the pressure of the job. If your body is in shape, it develops muscle and strength that carries over into your work life where you can withstand a hard day on the job, have a clear head, and problem-solve so that there need not be a repeat of the hard day.

Your mental well-being is very much needed to have a clear mind to engage the brain. Operating on all cylinders is needed for problem-solving, analytical thinking, critical thinking, conflict negotiating, communication, collaboration, cooperation, and social interactions that are positive and fruitful.

Your spiritual well-being is very important too. You may not think so, but science has also shown us how powerful faith can be in our lives, especially when storms of life occur. Having the faith that you will safely and securely weather the storm and come out of it positively gets you through many moments when fear, doubt, and unbelief try to manipulate your thoughts and your will. It is at those times knowing you are not alone; there is a positive outcome on the other side that keeps hope alive. With hope, the perseverance to get through the storm and get to the other side is strong and unwaverable.

AN INVITATION TO JOIN US

Join us and become a member of the Future Forward Academy and be a part of a community that lives in hope and prepares for the future with the faith and belief that the compass for us is leading us to our NorthStar.

Access our website and join our mailing list at
https://futureforwardacademy.com/

Access our Career Capsule Newsletter on LinkedIn at
https://tinyurl.com/CareerCapsuleNewsletter

Join our Membership Site TODAY!

(https://futureforwardacademymembers.com

Connect with us on LinkedIn:

https://www.linkedin.com/in/annamariabliven/

https://www.linkedin.com/in/drscottcpa/

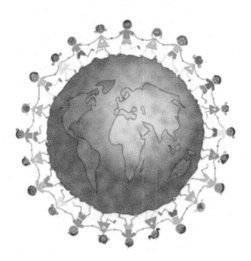

REFERENCES

Cherry, K. (2022, April 13) Alfred Binet and the history of IQ testing. *Very Well Mind.* https://www.verywellmind.com/history-of-intelligence-testing-2795581

CQ Model (n.d.) The CQ Model.com http://www.thecqmodel.com/

Cuncic, A. (2022, November 17) What is imposter syndrome? Very Well Mind. https://www.verywellmind.com/imposter-syndrome-and-social-anxiety-disorder-4156469

Earley, P.C. and Mosakowski, E. (2004, October) Cultural Intelligence. *Harvard Business Review.* https://hbr.org/2004/10/cultural-intelligence

Farrell, J. (2023) What is cultural intelligence? EwGroup. [Blog] https://theewgroup.com/us/blog/what-is-cultural-intelligence/

Hutchinson, A. (2022, November 10) Which social platforms work best for each industry? *Social Media Today.* [Infographic] https://www.socialmediatoday.com/news/Best-Social-Platforms-by-Industry-Infographic/636331/

Project management statistics: Trends and common mistakes in 2022 (2023) *Team Stage* [Blog] https://teamstage.io/project-management-statistics/

Roth, J.D. (2018, April 15) How to find your purpose in life: 12 powerful exercises to help you discover purpose and passion. *Get Rich Slowly.* https://www.getrichslowly.org/finding-purpose/

Schwantes, M. (2023) 5 Simple ways to discover your life's purpose: Find your purpose with these techniques. *Inc.com.* https://www.inc.com/marcel-schwantes/five-simple-exercises-to-find-your-life-purpose.html

Schwantes, M. (2023) Science says only 8 percent of people actually achieve their goals: Here are 7 things they do differently. *Inc.com.* https://www.inc.com/marcel-schwantes/science-says-only-8-percent-of-people-actually-achieve-their-goals-here-are-7-things-they-do-differently.html

Thi, E.L. (2007). Adversity quotient in predicting job performance viewed through the perspective of the big five. https://core.ac.uk/download/pdf/30860559.pdf

Thottam, I. (2023) Social media mistakes that can disqualify you from a job. *Monster.com.* https://www.monster.com/career-advice/article/these-social-media-mistakes-can-actually-disqualify-you-from-a-job

Viswanath, P. (2020, July 29) How does adversity quotient

define ones ability to endure? Psych Logs. https://www.psychologs.com/article/how-does-adversity-quotient-define-ones-ability-to-endure

Why emotional intelligence makes you more successful La Trobe University Nest. (2023) [Blog] https://www.latrobe.edu.au/nest/why-emotional-intelligence-makes-you-more-successful/#:~:text=Emotional%20intelligence%20is%20the%20ability,conflict%20and%20improve%20job%20satisfaction

Having a life well-balanced and one that you LOVE

ABOUT THE AUTHORS

Dr. Scott Dell is an active academic, recovering CPA, lifelong learner, enthusiastic teacher, experienced entrepreneur, motivating coach, successful author, and proud Navy veteran. He brings practical experience in the career space having interviewed and hired 1,000's. He is the author of the definitive LinkedIn resource "Your COMPLETE Guide to SUCCEEDING with LinkedIn". Dr. Scott is also a keynote speaker about Generative Artificial Intelligence helping users, from corporations such as Rolls Royce to universities such as USC, apply this powerful technology for a wide variety of applications. Subscribe to his Career Capsule newsletter, providing tips and tricks and GAI insights to help HR professionals and job seekers succeed in their job search and life at https://tinyurl.com/CareerCapsuleNewsletter.

Dr. AnnaMaria Bliven holds a Doctorate in Business Administration (DBA) from the University of Wisconsin-Whitewater College of Business and Economics and an experienced business owner, non-profit organization founder, leader, and educator. Dr. B. is also an active entrepreneur, manager, learner, published author, guest speaker, Army veteran, and business professional. She has experience owning, operating, and growing businesses and organizations. Her passion for business and education has led her to help inspire others to take the steps needed to fulfill their dreams and passions. This includes guiding and assisting people to work at home as remote workers, establish new businesses and organizations, assist with the writing, editing, and publishing of their books, and lead the way for being the solution to underserved populations left out of online, remote job opportunities. Being a "Champion for Changed Lives," she works tirelessly on initiatives to even the playing field for the DIS-Community: disadvantaged, disempowered, and disenchanted.

Made in the USA
Columbia, SC
05 February 2024

31096137R00134